Why Love is not Enough

Sol Gordon, Ph.D.

BOB ADAMS, INC.
PUBLISHERS

Why Love is not Enough

Sol Gordon, Ph.D.

BOB ADAMS, INC.
P U B L I S H E R S

Published by

Bob Adams Inc
840 Summer Street
Boston, Massachusetts 02127

ISBN 1-55850-960-7

Manufactured in the United States of America.

1 2 3 4 5 6 7 8 9 10

Cover design by Giselle deGuzman.

Dedication

On December 4th of this year, my wife Judith and I celebrated our 35th wedding anniversary. Along with our misfortunes, we've experienced many joys and great times. My marriage to Judith was the best thing that ever happened to me — and it's still happening!

Judith, thanks for your patience with me; thanks for being yourself. I hope that when we celebrate our 50th anniversary together, we'll look up and say to each other, "I still like you."

Acknowledgments

Many thanks are due to Tom Burney, who took my longhand manuscript and entered it into his computer in the early stages of the book's composition; and to Brandon Toropov, my editor at Bob Adams, Inc., who shaped the book during its final stages

Contents

Why Love is not Enough

Sol Gordon, Ph.D.

BOB ADAMS, INC.
PUBLISHERS

Introduction

This book is for people who want to find and encourage the growth of a lasting, mature relationship—whether for the first time or not.

If you've: accepted even the least promising invitations; been on innumerable awkward and frustrating "blind dates"; followed all the leads supplied in the magazines for "meeting the right person"; dressed up or down for every imaginable occasion; bought a dog so you could walk it; spent too much time in singles bars; wandered through the supermarkets hoping to meet someone; "borrowed" a child for the obligatory trip to the zoo; made a lot of eye contact at parties; gone first class on business trips in the hopes of meeting an interesting fellow traveler; tried desperately to become knowledgeable about certain topics that seem to interest the opposite sex; or simply fantasized about hooking up, somehow, with Mr. or Ms. Right . . . all without any tangible results . . . read on.

Perhaps, if you're a woman, you're beginning to believe that all the nice men are either married or gay. The rest, or so the conventional wisdom goes, are all too ugly, too short, too old, too young, too "wimpy," or flat-out insensitive and interested only in sex.

If you're a man, you may think that all the available women are too unattractive, too smart, too dumb, too materialistic, or, to quote the ancient (and crude) complaint, "unwilling to put out."

Yet there is someone for just about everyone, and something close to 90 percent of us, it's estimated, eventually marry—certainly an encouraging sign for those eager to enter into a long-term relationship.

In this book, I will encourage you to start with a whole new attitude. Many of us begin our relationships with others from positions of self-doubt, desperation, and low self-esteem . . . which, when you think about it, aren't the most attractive traits to display to a potential partner.

What must you do? Make up your mind that you want a positive, enriching relationship, and this book will help you in your efforts.

By "successful," I really don't mean anything fancy. My definition of a successful relationship is one in which, after the passage of a considerable period of time, the partners can still look up and say to each other, "I like you."

The guidelines in this book are simple; the actual follow-through, however, will be difficult, and will require that you supply time and patience. You should also try to cultivate an outlook that allows you to give new approaches an honest try. You may not agree with all of my suggestions, but you should try to keep an open mind.

Following are some basic principles that underlie the ideas in this book. They apply whether or not you've been married previously, and whether you're male or female.

If you're desperate, you give off negative vibrations. You become unattractive no matter how you look.

Feelings of self-worth should not depend on finding someone as a partner. If you feel you don't amount to anything unless you "catch" someone, you probably won't amount to much after you do.

If you honestly believe that life has passed you by, the odds are that it has. No matter the barriers (including physical handicap and previous relationship problems) you can find someone who'll help you grow into a happier, more complete person.

Sex is not the most important element in a relationship. Intimacy is more of an authentic turn-on, and of the ten most important aspects of a mature relationship, sex, in my view, ranks ninth.

Some love relationships are mature; others are immature. And it's easier than you think to tell the difference.

Successful relationships involve compromises and are almost never ideal. They're often enjoyable, but expecting them to be so all of the time is unrealistic.

Mutal commitment to growth is an essential component of a happy relationship. That means growth as a couple as well as each partner's growth as an individual.

Marriage should be a rational, intellectually sound decision. If you think you've found the right person, the best advice is always to think again. There are very definitely some people you should not marry. Though powerful love feelings and sexual attraction often play major roles, a marriage stands little or no chance of succeeding if the issues surrounding it aren't thought through fully.

* * *

This book offers no guarantees or panaceas. Nothing works for everyone, but the approaches I offer here can help you learn about a new, realistic way of looking at yourself and your relationships with others. Once you've done that, you can use my suggestions to help you judge whether your relationship is mature enough for a marriage commitment.

I wrote this book for intelligent people eager to make up their own minds about how to live and what risks are worth taking in relationships. If this describes you, I feel it's worth your while to keep reading.

Together, you and I might make a *shiddoch* (Yiddish for "marital match or agreement"). No, I'm not asking you to "marry" me — I'm asking you to approach this book realizing that work is required on your part. My end of the bargain is to provide you with some good ideas; yours is to begin by considering yourself worth spending time with, and then to be ready and willing to try the new approaches that can change your life.

S.G.
June, 1988

Chapter One:
Creating The New You

ARE YOU READY for a mature relationship?

The answer to that question depends, in large measure, on the answer to a great many other ones, the most important of which is: Are you a self-accepting person, or a self-defeating one?

To be sure, everyone has problems. Each of us has areas of inadequacy. But the real question is, how do you approach the complex maze of attitudes, predispositions, thoughts, feelings, and past history that is "you"? Are you determined to put your best foot forward . . . or are you more likely not to give yourself the benefit of the doubt?

If you aren't sure who you are, if you don't feel good about that person, you cannot expect someone else to do so. It's as simple as that. If you want to wind up in a challenging, mature, adult relationship—and certainly if you want to get married—you must have a very good idea of what can be expected from the person with whom your potential partner will be spending all that time.

The vast majority of the ideas I'll present here will be designed to help you achieve two main goals. The first is to help you implement strategies for establishing a wholesome, non-narcissistic confidence in your identity. The second is to build on that self-knowledge in a mature, enriching relationship—the kind that must, like all real-life experiences, eventually deal with the unavoidable problems and challenges of everyday life. Immature love – either the egocentric kind we focus on ourselves, or the all-encompassing whoosh of passion and infatuation with which many relationships begin – simply will not stand the test of time in a long-term relationship. That's why this book is called *Why Love Is Not Enough*.

Some Danger Signs

Would you want to go out with yourself if you called your house some evening and asked yourself for a date?

Before you answer, think about what kind of image you present. Are you lonely? Anxious? Worried that it's too late for you to "get" someone? Do you feel that the sooner you get married, the better off you'll be? Do you want to "find someone *soon*"? Are you, to put it bluntly, desperate?

If you want to stay that way, don't make any effort to change at all. Proceed with your usual methods. Take whatever hasn't worked (the singles bars, the classifieds, the uninspiring blind dates) and keep trying frantically. You may even want to try some new things that won't work: astrology, tarot cards, tea leaves, or renting billboard space to publicize your phone number.

Or you can accentuate the positive, begin from the proposition that you are a good person, and proceed to address the question of your relationships with others by honestly asking yourself what you can do to become a better, happier individual. Someone *you* like.

Obviously, my advice is to consider the latter option. Take a personal inventory, see what it is you're presenting to the outside world in general and to potential partners specifically, and make some sober assessments. It may take some time, so if you are looking for instant solutions, you may find the rest of this book unsatisfying. There are no quick answers to the question of how best to initiate a satisfying, mature relationship.

Thankfully, though, the answers that are available will, if acted upon, probably make you a happier person.

How To Feel Better About Yourself

If you're still with me, and you agree that the second option is preferable to the first, here's my plan. It incorporates some concrete, long-term suggestions for making yourself more appealing and, most important, heightening your own self-esteem.

Give up the meat markets. Entirely. No more singles bars, blind dates, or pickup discos. You should begin to view others as what they are—individuals—and not conquests. By the same token, there's no reason, once you've determined that your objective is to enter a mature relationship, you should show up at these places. (Exceptions: singles nights sponsored by your church or synagogue or similar groups, or groups you attend to cultivate a new or passionate interest, such as book, travel, or nature clubs.)

Make a vow to take part in no casual sex. That means no sex with anyone you feel has not made a commitment. Severe? Not really. If you are genuinely determined to wind up in a mature relationship, there's no longer any reason to put yourself in the no-win, short-term position of being someone else's "experience." Tennessee Williams once said that the reason so many women are willing to risk sex with anybody is because of the possibility of love. As his plays often reveal, the risk frequently does not pay off.

For men, motivations underlying casual sex tend to incorporate another idea entirely called "scoring." What many men fail to realize, however, is that their "scores" are often the very reason they find it difficult to develop long-standing relationships and/or successful marriages. They get a lot of practice making out and less practice making sense of their encounters.

In our society, people often use sex merely as a way to prove their masculinity or femininity, or as a tactic to *avoid* intimacy. (How's that for a paradox?) Consequently, many people—particularly single women—have found that sex with someone whom they don't really know often fulfills only the short-term partner's objectives. The simple fact is, the very best way to gauge the strength and depth of any possible love relationship is to hold off having sex—whether you're male or female. (These days, of course, there is also the very real incentive of making sure you don't die of a sexually transmitted disease, another potent argument in favor of searing off one-night stands. I'll discuss this issue in much greater detail later on in the book.)

That's all very well, you may be saying to yourself, but just what am I supposed to do in the meantime? First, realize that frequent sex is not a physical requirement, and that you are unlikely to develop psychological problems from not "getting enough." Second, accept that your feelings are genuine, understandable, and natural—and, for heaven's sake, don't feel guilty about wanting to go to bed with someone. Third, don't be afraid to masturbate. Age is no impediment here; if you need some creative ideas on this score, read Betty Dodson's fine book *Sex For One: The Joy Of Selfloving* (Crown, 1987).

Tackle depression head-on. Let's face it. If you are reading this book, you're probably looking for a way to make your existing, and perhaps unsatisfying relationship more satisfying—or find someone altogether new to fill what you may feel is a void in your life. If it's the first case, you probably get depressed from time to time. And, of course, if it's the second case, you probably get depressed from time to time.

What do you usually do when you're depressed? (I'm referring here to "normal" depression occurring as a result of unhappy times and experiences, not to the kind that lasts for weeks and months regardless of circumstances—possibly requiring medical care.)

Many people respond to depression by giving themselves permission to eat too much. Or have a few too many drinks. Or go on spending sprees. Or gamble. Or smoke a joint. Before you follow any of these paths yourself, stop and try something new.

Go to the refrigerator. Find something sweet to eat and consume three or four non-compulsive mouthfuls. That will elevate your blood sugar level and give you, without too much difficulty, at least two "up" minutes.

Now. During those two minutes, *learn something new.* Look up four new words in the dictionary. Go to that unread book you've had on the shelf for two years. Learn a magic trick. Select a brand new recipe to show off. Call up a friend and ask what's new—and if the response is "Aah, not much," hang up right away and call someone else.

Be ruthless about learning something absolutely fresh and exciting during those two minutes. There's nothing more energizing than finding out something new—and there's virtually nothing more exhausting than being depressed.

Please don't misunderstand me. It's perfectly okay to be depressed at times. Life is often full of disappointing developments, grief, and tragic occurrences. But the message I hope I've gotten across here can go a long way toward helping you deal with such periods. That message is: Learning something new is an energizing, uplifting experience. Take advantage of that experience whenever you can.

Find a passion. Enhance your talents and skills in an area you've neglected up to this point. Every person can profit from a passionate interest, an exciting hobby, and, last but not least, the opportunity to show off a creative talent.

There are a number of ways to accomplish this goal. Obviously, you can study—take courses at your local community college, for instance. Or you might join a special interest, charitable, or community group that reflects something about which you have strong feelings. It could focus on any number of pursuits: environmental issues, public television, volunteering, wildlife preservation, anti-nuclear advocacy, church- or synagogue-related activities . . . the list is endless.

Alternatively, you might set specific long-term goals for yourself and follow them up just as enthusiastically. You could learn a new language—and reward yourself by taking your next vacation to a foreign country where the language is spoken! Learn to play badminton. Take up a musical instrument. *Take it seriously and give your efforts the time they need.* Whatever you select, do it well.

Why take the trouble? The reason's very simple. *If you have an interest, someone will eventually be interested in you.* Shared activities are the very best way to make new friends.

Do mitzvahs. What is a mitzvah? A biblical injunction to do good deeds. In contemporary usage, its practical definition would be something along the lines of "doing something good without any expectation of compensation in return."

A mitzvah is *not:* donating money to a charity and deducting the amount from your income tax return. A mitzvah is *not:* something you remind someone of relentlessly after it's completed. A mitzvah is *not:* being temporarily accommodating to friends or associates in the hope that they'll eventually like you and do favors for you.

Mitzvahs represent another potent weapon for tackling the problems of depression, unhappiness, and loneliness. Try it and see. Volunteer in a hospital; work with the homeless; become a Big Brother or Sister. (Call up your local United Way office or other volunteer center if you need more ideas.) In short, be helpful to someone who is more needy or vulnerable than you are.

If you are not ready for this because something terrible (such as the death of a loved one, for instance, or victimization in a violent crime) has taken place in your life, there are other options open to you. Join a support group which relates to your life experiences. Almost every city has dozens of such groups, and there's probably one which addresses your problem directly. In this way you can be helpful to others who are in similar situations, and still reap the benefits of "mitzvah therapy."

If that doesn't work, you might want to consider counseling as a valuable tool for examining your reaction to the difficult events in your life. Therapy will help you find out what's blocking your emotional progress or causing you to make the same mistakes repeatedly. For most run-of-the-mill neurotics (i.e., just about all of us, excluding the mentally ill) it shouldn't take long to notice results. You should be able to see some progress in terms of your own personal insights within about ten sessions, as long as you work with a counselor or therapist you like and respect. (If you *don't* like and respect the therapist, find another.)

If you're not in shape, get yourself into shape. Schedule yourself for a full physical, and then make modest starts in the following areas.

> *Exercise regularly.* Try to set up a workable plan with your doctor. At the very least, go for long walks regularly

> *Control your weight.* Reduce your sugar and red meat intake, and make every effort to swear off fast food and deep-fried menu items.

> *Stop smoking.* If you smoke, you will be happier, healthier, and more attractive to others once you stop. So stop. (I know, I know—it's easier said than done.)

> *Attend a health club.* Joining a health club is an excellent way to formalize your commitment to the "new you"—and it's not a bad way to meet new people, either.

Improve your personality. This may sound all-encompassing, but it is a real goal you should set for yourself, and one which you can achieve. (Obviously, not all the following suggestions will apply to you.)

You might start by dressing and looking as well as you possibly can. This will not only improve your standing with others, but it will also radically alter the way you feel about yourself.

Another good idea is to make a promise never again to say anything negative about yourself to anyone you meet. Reserve moderate self-criticism for the conversations you hold with your mirror or with your very closest friends. The fact is, self-deprecation is very boring to others. Even passing along the various injustices visited on you by the world at large should be an activity you share with people you know well and trust to hold your confidence. How interested are *you* when a co-worker moans about how he should be making more money at his age, or how hard it is for him to manage with prices so high?

Here's another tip: proceed from the central idea that you're a nice person. Even if you don't believe it, pretend, or, as the old saying has it, "Fake it until you can make it." Start by saying "thank you" loud and clear when you receive a compliment. The same "faking it" approach will work wonders when it comes to developing a sense of humor. If you have to, start by laughing when you hear other people doing so. (Remember, the ability to laugh at oneself is one of the most important aspects of an attractive person.)

Along the same lines, you should be quite generous in your (legitimate and believable) compliments directed toward others. Feel free to say things like, "That's a nice shirt," "You look good today," or "What a lovely dress." As my mother used to say, "Zug a gut wort, es kost nit mehr." ("Say a good word, it doesn't cost more.") But be careful not to earn a reputation as an insincere person—don't go overboard.

Be optimistic if it kills you. It won't, but too many people act as though it might. Often, being optimistic begins with the simple decision not to bring a negative attitude to the proceedings. For instance, avoid peppering yourself and your associates with the phrases "have to," "gotta," and "should've." These phrases carry negative, pessimistic connotations—they imply you're unsatisfied with what has happened or is about to take place.

If you must undertake something you're not crazy about, do it with a smile on your face if at all possible. There's very little in life that doesn't present options of greater and lesser attractiveness. Make the best of your situation.

Improve your current relationships. Pay special attention to your relationships with parents and siblings. Try afresh to keep the lines of communication open with positive messages—but don't expect to work miracles on the first phone call.

Where family members are concerned, be especially polite. If things have been strained in the past, politeness will keep the relationship functioning and perhaps provide you with needed distance. Love is nice in family relationships, but if it's lacking, settle for politeness—and love may come gradually.

Be prepared to try forgiveness. One proven approach is to take the initiative, contact someone who's hurt you, and offer to bury the hatchet. Alternatively, you might ask forgiveness of at least one person whom you feel you have hurt in the past. This approach can yield surprisingly rapid results. The reason? Hostility, jealousy, and the desire for revenge all use up energy—energy you need for personal growth.

Remember the words of the famous American psychologist William James: "Wisdom is learning what to overlook." Perhaps your long-held grudge is standing in the way of your own development as a person—and your healthy relationships with others.

Of course, you *will* have to stand up for some things, otherwise you'll be taken advantage of and run the risk of becoming trapped in victimizing situations. Nevertheless, try to strike a balance. In your relationships with family members and the world at large, try not to take everything seriously. The truth is, most of the things people get all worked up over matter very little. By all means, set your priorities, and stick to them—but don't be afraid to forgive sometimes.

Concentrate on same-sex friends. My experience is that people who can't make same-sex friends become very poor marital partners. If your aim is to initiate a positive, long-term relationship, you should realize from the beginning that lovers come and go, but best friends last forever.

Cultivating same-sex friends is a very good way to develop your capacity for long-term, mature relationships. When you can honestly say, "Someone like me thinks I'm a good person and enjoys my company," you'll eventually conclude that you are likeable enough to be attractive to the opposite sex. (These dynamics are not the same in a homosexual relationship.)

When it comes to making new friends, take some risks. Unless you are willing to risk rejection, you are not likely to find acceptance. Mutual trust comes along the way, but not necessarily at the beginning. Without an initial risk, nothing much happens.

It may help to bear in mind that failure is an event, not a person. As Eleanor Roosevelt put it, "No one can make you feel inferior without your consent." This isn't a cheap, sentimental slogan; it should form the basis for a lifelong goal about how you look at your life.

Improve your intellect and broaden your horizons. Read a newspaper every day for at least 20 minutes. Read *The New York Times* on Sunday.

Watch public television regularly. Swear off junk television, or limit your intake to one mindless program per week. (You'll look forward to it more.) There is a lot of garbage on television. The more of it you watch, the more boring you'll become.

Try to read one self-help book per month. (Starting with this one, of course.) You'll find a full index of recommended titles at the rear of this book.

Some Complications

You are, by now, probably wondering, "Where on earth am I going to get the time to do all these things?" The answer is: it will be tough. Try isolating one or two activities and doing them for twenty-one days. That way they'll become habits, ingrained parts of your life. Then you'll be free to move on to new challenges, and, over time, you can—I promise—address them all. As the old nursery rhyme advises, "One thing at a time, and that done well, is a very good rule, as many can tell."

Remember, though, that energy is mainly psychological, and

that the process of *not* learning is exhausting. If you have nothing to look forward to after work, you'll be tired when you're finished working. Time and energy are easy to come by for those people who have a sense of purpose and dare to be optimistic. Their energy is often *generated* — not consumed — by pursuing meaningful goals. And they hardly ever fuss about being busy and not having enough time.

The whole process will take some time. Certainly a number of months, and perhaps as long as a year. This raises an important question. While you're busy developing the "new you," what do you do about all the people who are used to the "old you"? If you share activities and interests with certain friends or family members, and you suddenly find yourself altering those activities (perhaps because you feel they're impeding your growth), how do you deal with the inevitable pressure to go back to the "good old days"?

My advice is to be honest, and, tactfully, to let the other person in on the fact that the "good old days" didn't do you much good. Come right out and say that you're taking time to put your life in order. By acknowledging that you're looking for new strategies for self-fulfillment, you'll be able to open yourself up to constructive criticisms and suggestions.

Accepting that criticism will require no small amount of tact and courage on your part, and you should know in advance that most of what others say *won't* be constructive. Nevertheless, keep an open mind, and note what's helpful. Openness to criticism without getting hurt or becoming defensive is a calculated risk, but it could pay off handsomely. After all, these are the people who know you best!

And how about responding to people you just plain don't like? That's easy. Say as little as possible, don't get mad, and remember to smile a lot.

Patience

Don't get desperate. Be patient. Try to make yourself happier and more confident by following the suggestions I've outlined in this chapter. You'll eventually meet people you like.

Try, wherever possible, to do this in a "non-date" setting. Ask a friend to invite you and an "eligible" to a casual home dinner. Don't rush things. Meet first, consider the serious stuff later. And remember, no one-night stands.

Now is the time to be nice to yourself. Don't be afraid of what might happen. Take the risk. Start thinking of yourself as someone worth knowing. Eventually someone else will think of you in the same way.

Chapter Two: Love — It Comes In Two Varieties

LET'S TALK about love.

Love is, admittedly, a difficult idea to define precisely, much less explain in detail. Yet just about everyone would agree that a good relationship, and certainly a good marriage, should have a component of love in it. As a person who hopes to enter such a relationship, you probably hope that your partner will love you, and that you will be able to love your partner — whether or not you feel that you've come to a full understanding of the meaning of the verb "to love."

Many of us get muddled when we start trying to "nail down" what love is. Part of the reason is that, when it comes to love, many people simply feel so insecure about the matter that they don't know *what* they should expect. Often, the only guides provided by our culture are mass media stereotypes and the over-romanticized visions of love we picked up during adolescence.

In addition, many of us come to the conclusion that being in love presupposes some degree of insanity. If you're really in love, the theory goes, you are, by definition, slightly paralyzed and more or less unable to function in the outside world. Is love really like that? If so, do we really want to be "in" it?

Looking At Love In A New Way

What is love? What's most important in a loving relationship? How can you tell if you're really in love?

Let's begin at the beginning. Though love may be difficult to define, it is certainly an important part of virtually everyone's life.

And for my part, I believe that if you feel you're in love, then you are. But there's a catch: though you may be in love with someone, it is incumbent upon you to ask what *kind* of love it is. The answer to that question can say a great deal about your relationship's long-term potential.

There are two kinds of love: mature and immature. And neither term refers to age. The mere fact that someone's entered his or her later years is no guarantee of maturity.

The sheer volume of failed third and fourth marriages should be enough to convince just about anyone that previous life experiences do not guarantee that a person has gained the capacity for mature love.

But what *is* mature love? You probably already know without realizing it, because the two types are very easy to distinguish. Mature love is energizing; immature love is exhausting.

In a mature love relationship, you find yourself full of energy, ready to tackle new challenges and push back the boundaries that define what's possible. As important as this energy is in youthful relationships, it becomes even more essential in later life. (One of the nicest things about mature love is that, for older partners, it can offer serenity while still providing an important measure of vitality and excitement.)

Wonderful things happen when you're involved in a mature relationship. You genuinely enjoy your partner's company. You have time to do almost everything you want. You fulfill your responsibilities and are happy to do so. You tend to get along well with family and friends. Occasionally, of course, you have arguments with your partner, but not that much. You want to please each other.

All of this stands in marked contrast to what immature love has to offer. You probably can supply the examples yourself, either from your life or someone else's. In this type of relationship, you're tired most of the time. You procrastinate a lot. You tend to have problems at work. Your relationships with others — friends, siblings, parents — seem to require constant fence-mending. Perhaps domestic responsibilities are difficult for you to fulfill. ("Me? Wash the dishes? I can't do that! I'm in love!")

In an immature love situation, you may even be involved in what's known as a "hostile-dependent" relationship, in which you can't stand being without the person you supposedly love so deeply, pine after him or her in the face of even short periods of time apart — yet fight and argue with your partner most of the time when you are together. Mood swings, accusations of jealousy, and perhaps even violent actions mark the relationship.

How You Treat Your Partner, How Your Partner Treats You

Another clear difference between mature and immature love shows itself in the way the partners in a relationship decide to treat each other. People in mature love relationships tend to make an effort to be nice; people in immature love situations don't consider the implications of their remarks or actions on the long-term health of the relationship, and are often needlessly bitter, mean-spirited or selfish.

Consider the following dialogues, the first representing an exchange in an immature relationship, and the second representing the same situation resolved more constructively in a mature love setting.

Paul: Honey, let's have sex.

Erica: I have a headache. . .

Paul: You have a headache. On my day off. You have a lot of nerve!

John: Honey, let's have sex.

Robin: I have a headache. . .

John: I'm sorry you have a headache. I'll get you an aspirin. There's always tomorrow.

Security and Commitment to Mutual Growth

One of the most satisfying things mature love leads to is a sense of security—the kind of security that comes from the knowledge that you've found a partner whom you can count on in emergencies, during illnesses, or when you're under a great deal of stress. There is genuine comfort in discovering someone with the capacity to share in both your dreams *and* your defeats, and this kind of security is perhaps the most important characteristic of a stable, long-lasting love relationship.

In a mature love relationship, partners aren't threatened by each other's success or achievements. Rather, they're committed to mutual growth, and have a vested interest in the intellectual and emotional development of the other person, even if it means that some of the growth occurs outside the framework of the relationship.

Your partner may be a member of a study group that meets when you are busy, may frequently visit a friend without you, or may develop an interest in which you are unable or unwilling to participate. By the same token, you may want to take a course that helps you develop a favorite hobby, set up a work or volunteering schedule that doesn't include your partner, or simply make regular time for yourself at a favorite cafe or restaurant. None of these developments will be threatening to a mature relationship, because mature love partners are proud of each other's interests and achievements—and realize that, in the long run, these things indirectly benefit both parties by encouraging a challenging, rewarding marriage.

The immature relationship, however, is usually characterized by insecurity, tension, impetuousness, uncertainty, frequent fights, frequent "make-ups," and impressive measures of lust, infatuation, and low self-esteem. If one partner achieves something significant, the other may easily feel threatened and become depressed. Such developments will eventually rise to the surface, and one or, more likely, both of the partners may be confronted by serious self-esteem problems.

People in immature relationships may often find themselves peppered with awkward questions such as, "Do you love me?" "Do you *really* love me?" "Do you love me more than you loved (name of a former lover)?" (When such queries are a constant component of the relationship, my advice is to answer "no" and see what happens. Doing so will almost certainly do one or more of three things: get a more interesting conversation going; shock the questioner into looking at him or herself; or encourage both partners to talk about the relationship honestly.)

Promises, Promises

Does this sound familiar?

"Don't worry, honey, when we get married, I'll stop fooling around. You know you're the only one for me."

"I'm never going to get drunk again. I swear it. I've learned my lesson. (Two months later:) I'm never going to get drunk again. I swear it. I've learned my lesson."

"Please don't leave. I promise I'll stop gambling, just don't go away."

Immature love is full of promises. When the promises cover

up personal problems or habitual self-destructive behavior, there can be trouble. When the promises form the basis of a decision either to continue a relationship or to make a lifetime commitment, there can be big trouble.

The plain fact is, a bad situation is *always* made worse by marriage. To be sure, people change, and personal habits can be turned around—but when you've heard the same line several times, with no noticeable change in your partner's behavior, it's time to take a good long look at the relationship.

Mature love seems to depend far less than immature love on promises to atone and pleas for belief in a partner's having turned over a new leaf. Mature lovers know each other, and, by extension, don't require constant reassurance of a partner's newfound virtue. When there are challenges to the relationship—as there inevitably are—each side examines the problem as a knowledgeable participant in the ongoing process of building a life together, and not as a salesperson approaching a wary customer who, with a little better pitch, may eventually be induced to purchase a questionable product.

Is It Infatuation?

Let's assume that you're in the beginning stages of a new relationship. How will you be able to tell whether you have an immature and infatuation-based relationship or a potential mature love that deserves (and can support) a commitment from you and your partner?

During the first few weeks of the relationship, the two types may be virtually indistinguishable. But after this intense preliminary period (which can last as long as a month, and perhaps longer in the summertime), some differences will emerge.

If it's infatuation, the couple's intense feeling will begin to go sour, and some bitterness may even emerge. Suddenly, as you get to know each other a little better, the other person may no longer seem as perfect, appealing, or easy to talk to. For at least one of the partners, love begins to feel like something of a burden.

In addition, people in immature relationships tend, more and more, not to care what the other person thinks about them. (Indeed, many wind up unconcerned about what *anyone* thinks about them.) They may neglect their studies or their work; they may be careless about their appearance; they may quickly become jealous, irritable, or petty with their partners; and they may neglect important responsibilities. The general feeling surrounding the relationship is generally one of boredom.

In a relationship that has the potential for mature love, however, the process of becoming better acquainted with each other continues to be enjoyable and exciting. As knowledge and feelings about the partner grow stronger, there is a sense of a deepening relationship. The more you get to know the other person, the more you find to like and admire. Usually, relationships in which the early stages are successfully negotiated provide the kind of environment in which each person feels he or she wants to be the best possible partner for the loved one.

Eventually, people in mature relationships are inspired: to take extra pains with work or studies; to groom themselves carefully and look as appealing as possible for their partner; or simply to put forth the best aspects of their personalities. In short, they express their love by trying in every possible way to make themselves better persons, thereby becoming more worthy of the love they want to receive.

What Some People Say About Love. . .
And What You Could Say In Response

If you loved me, you'd sleep with me. If you loved me, you wouldn't make demands like that. (Sex is never a test or proof of love, and you can't "buy" love with sex. Unfortunately, it's still true that many women have sex because of the possibility of love, while many men have sex because of the possibilities of sex. Remember that sex is frequently confused with love, and that there are happy couples who love each other a great deal with what some might consider inadequate sex lives.)

If you have sex before marriage, you'll have nothing to look forward to and all the surprise will be removed from your relationship. If sex is the only surprise in marriage, then no one should get married. (Frankly, sex alone is not worth it.)

Love is blind. For twenty-four hours. (Then you have to open your eyes.)

Stand by your man (or woman). Sure, but stand up for yourself, too. (If someone forces sex on you, consistently makes impossible demands, or beats you up, that has nothing to do with love, no matter what anyone says. More likely explanations for such behavior: insensitivity, neurosis, dependency, or fear.)

You "really" fall in love only once in a lifetime. Nonsense. (Though a good argument can be made against the possibility of being genuinely "in love" with more than one person at a time, even the most intense love affair may be followed by another relationship that stands or falls on its own merits. That relationship may be even more deeply rooted and emotionally satisfying than the one preceding it. Along the same lines, bear in mind that your world will not end if a relationship does. Mature love is a shared experience; when someone does not return your affections, do your best to deal with the natural disappointment, but accept that other relationships may be just as rewarding.)

Keep a stopwatch on your partner and get every bit of time from him or her that you have coming. It's the only way you can really feel good about yourself or your relationship. Requiring constant attention and

"T.L.C." is not the mark of a mature relationship. (But you *can* like yourself more by putting yourself "in the presence" of your partner—something you can do whether you are together or not.)

Love comes only to the "beautiful people." Mature love is not determined by looks, income level, or social status. (People who have a good measure of self-esteem are attractive to *some* other people. Period. Everyone is unique; everyone's life can be enriched on some level by love. Don't ask the cosmetic and toiletries manufacturers what they have to say about this; they have a vested interest in getting you to believe that perfumes, hair tonics, vaginal sprays, and wrinkle cream will make all the difference in your life. They're not telling the truth. By the way, have you ever noticed how few "Hollywood-type" and "meant for each other" relationships last?)

The Signs of a Mature Love Relationship

Erich Fromm, in his classic *The Art of Loving,* describes his four criteria that characterize a mature love relationship. According to Fromm, in such a relationship both partners care for the other person, respect each other, assume responsibility for each other, and develop joint understanding.

Another good yardstick is put forward by Robert J. Sternberg, professor of psychology at Yale University. Dr. Sternberg believes that the three most crucial ingredients in a successful relationship are commitment, intimacy, and passion.

Finally, we come to my list. My items are a little more extensive, and probably somewhat more pragmatic than the two I've mentioned, though obviously you're free to use all three in evaluating your relationships. Love is an inexact science—my wife, for instance, feels that the entry at number ten should in fact be listed as number two. You'll probably have your own standards. Use the list below as a starting point, not a final checklist.

I should say that, in any relationship, commitment is imperative. That element is so important that it underlies the entire list, and does not appear. If the relationship cannot encourage or sustain commitment, there's no point in making up a list in the first place.

That having been said, here is my list of the ten most important characteristics of a mature relationship.

One: Intimacy. Closeness and the ability to truly love and care for each other.

Two: A sense of humor. Willingness to laugh at oneself and the world at large. (If it is extremely difficult for you to develop a sense of humor, please do not plan on raising a family; laughter is a compulsory ingredient when it comes to having children.)

Three: Honest communication. Openness and good listening skills.

Four: A common sense of mission and purpose. Shared ethical and/or spiritual goals.

Five: Equality. A conscious sense of the essential importance of respect for each other as partners, and shared responsibility in career, leisure, childrearing, and lifestyle choices.

Six: A sense of adventure. A desire to keep the relationship fresh; new and interesting ways of expressing affection for each other.

Seven: Shared experience. An ever-growing repository of mutual undertakings, private conversations, and shared thoughts on issues and events, as well as celebrations, rituals, and traditions you both enjoy.

Eight: Respect for the other person's feelings and wishes. The willingness to delay one's own short-term desires in the knowledge that a similar willingness will exist on the part of the other person at a later time. Respect for the other's feelings and wishes regarding lovemaking.

Nine: Passion. Including, but not limited to, a healthy sex life.

Ten: Sharing in domestic duties. Not being limited by gender stereotypes; not allowing one partner to claim a monopoly on all household tasks for the purpose of taking on a "martyr" role. Accepting responsibility for doing one's fair share of the more unpleasant household tasks.

As I indicated earlier, the rankings are, to some degree, matters of individual taste and perception. Nevertheless, anything that makes it into the "top ten" is, by definition, of major significance in a relationship; I'd recommend thinking seriously and creatively about how and where the above guidelines can be incorporated into your life with your partner.

I have occasionally been criticized for not including financial security in the above list. I'd agree that this is an important factor, but I feel that that there are many, many successful relationships that thrive in an adverse financial environment. In my view, the justification for including this item on the top ten simply isn't there. Then again, it could be reasonably considered to be a strong candidate for Number Eleven on an extended list.

"Madly In Love"

For one neurotic reason or another, men and women sometimes fall hopelessly in love with people they don't even know very well, let alone like. Sometimes it becomes an obsession; nothing else on earth seems to matter except that one person. Like any other addiction, such an obsession can (and often does) become very destructive for all concerned. Sometimes people will fall madly in love with those who not only don't return the affection, but are outright hostile as well.

If there's simply no rational component to a love relationship, the odds are pretty stiff against its lasting for any period of time. In addition, it's not uncommon that "madly in love" becomes "tragically in love." More often than not, the love object is a fantasy. When the real person emerges, the disappointment and bitterness can be quite severe—perhaps even violently so.

On the other hand, sometimes people *back away* from relationships with others they really like—not simply as a result of   fear of commitment (a currently fashionable diagnosis for such problems), but often because they don't feel the intense passion, heat, or reckless abandon of "mad" love. (This very often occurs after a failed relationship or marriage which began "madly.")

In any case, my advice is not to try to settle down with someone you haven't really gotten to know (and certainly not to think about long-term commitment with someone you actually dislike, or who seems to dislike you) no matter how "crazy" you are about the person.

Changes

Needless to say, some relationships may start out immaturely and become mature later on. All relationships begin (and continue to grow) with elements of immaturity. That's why all marriages incorporate a certain amount of tension at any given moment. Marriages are about growth, and the very idea of growth necessitates a passage from a lesser degree of maturity to a greater one. There's really no reason that an immature element of a relationship, cannot, over time, undergo change, dramatic or radical. Such change can enrich both partners.

Still, the relationships that are the most durable, the ones I've called mature relationships here, usually have mutual commitment as their central and strongest component. Though every marriage will undergo changes in levels of intimacy, passion, communication, if the commitment is there, that's a very good sign for long term growth.

The fact that there is always some level of immaturity present in any relationship means that, for each partner, there is a certain amount of risk. But, having satisfied ourselves that the relationship itself is mature in nature, we must take that risk. My friend Leo Buscaglia, probably the world's foremost authority on love and loving, takes a very firm position on this subject.

Dr. Buscaglia argues again and again that those who want to love truly have no choice but simply to do so, without guarantees of reciprocation; they have no choice but to believe, accept, and trust . . . and hope that the love they give others will be returned. No guarantees. No assurances. Just the decision to love.

And that is the paradox. Even the mature relationship, the one grounded in commitment and founded on each partner's growth, has at its heart a certain instability. Such a relationship does not incorporate a mechanical, 50-50 division of emotional support, material contribution, or decision-making power and ability. No relationship can do this.

Mature love creates its own balance, with the partnership progressing through ever-changing, ever-challenging phases. One party may be in a dominant position in one area for a time, only to be followed by the other partner's ascension a little later. Love, like life itself, is a changing, fluid proposition. It cannot be negotiated finally or reduced to a cold set of equations. It must— and with flexibility, humility, and a healthy sense of humor, it can—be born, live, and thrive in a continuously changing interpersonal environment.

Chapter 3:
Before You Say, "I Do. . ."

YOU'VE DECIDED THAT you have a mature love relationship You may even want to get married. (I hope you'll agree that there's no point in marrying if the relationship is immature.) You're willing and able to "take the plunge." Now, however, is precisely the time to stop and think again.

These days, many if not most marriages are not successful ones. About half of all marriages break up in five years' time, and another ten percent probably should. The Census Bureau has estimated that of all women who have ever been married, 24 percent have had at least one divorce; the estimated figure for men is much higher. About 40 percent of all marriages that have taken place in the 1980s have been re-marriages. To be sure, the figures are sobering.

I'm not writing this to scare you out of getting married. Just because the statistics say that there is a high rate of divorce doesn't mean that your marriage will not be successful. And don't pay attention to the odds that you will end up getting a divorce if your parents divorced. Nothing is inevitable except death.

Specifically, don't "count yourself out" if you're a woman over the age of thirty looking for a serious relationship. As the media trumpets regularly, there are, broadly speaking, fewer single men available in this age group than we might like. . . but do you really want to let your self-image, your love life, and your future be determined by a bunch of statistics? You're a person, not a digit. Your life is determined by what you put into it; the external demographics may incline, but they cannot compel. (It's interesting to note that many of the early "scare studies" first publicized were founded on faulty statistical work; they didn't take into account the number of men who become available each year as a result of divorces.)*

The point is, statistics don't get married. People do. There are still quite a lot of real life examples of good marriages—even among couples with two sets of divorced parents, family histories of alcoholism, or any other profile you care to name.

My purpose here is to tell you why many contemporary marriages are not successful, in the hope that this knowledge might help you reflect on your own decision to marry a particular person and perhaps reevaluate that decision if you feel it's appropriate.

Of course, there are many reasons why marriages don't succeed. Often couples marry for the wrong reasons. The least rational motive for wanting to spend your life with someone is sex, and this overemphasis on sex constitutes a major reason for marital failure.

You can be sexually attracted to someone with whom you can't even hold a conversation. You could have an affair with someone you never address verbally. You can be sexually excited by *parts* of people. But you cannot expect to build a lasting, satisfying

---

*The good news for women on this front is that recent research indicates that the year 1987 was something of a turning point demographically. The overall pool of men (from which single men are drawn) is grown relative to the overall pool of women. The estimates are that, by 1990, there will be 108 men for every 100 women (as compared to 93 men for every 100 women in 1970).

relationship with someone in whom you have only sexual interests.

The next irrational reason is, surprisingly, love. Being "in love" is not enough of a reason to marry. Let me emphasize this. Love alone is no excuse for marriage, even if the relationship is a mature one. People who marry only or mainly for love (or because they're "crazy about each other," believe they have "a marriage made in heaven," think they're "meant for each other," are convinced it was "love at first sight," etc.), very seldom have successful marriages and more often than not separate or divorce.

Surprised? Many people are. Don't misunderstand me; it is perfectly natural and desirable to be sexually attracted and in love with the person you marry. But marriage is meant to be an intellectual and rational decision; you can be madly in love with someone who is totally unacceptable as a marriage partner, as experienced marriage counselors can confirm.

In marriage, the issue is not how much you are in love—or even how compatible you are, or what common interests you share. The real issue is, how are you going to deal with the inevitable incompatibilites that are part of any marriage? Consider the following scenarios, in which the apple of someone's eye turned out to be "someone else," often in a matter of months.

The strong, silent, romantic man you married has suddenly become morose and anxious after losing his "secure" job (or: after the birth of the first baby; or: after being forgiven for a discovered affair).

Your charming, loving, witty, and independent girlfriend has become a dependent, over-solicitous, complacent wife. Her independence was what attracted you most. Now that it's gone, she's driving you nuts, and you feel that your marriage is becoming increasingly boring.

The gracious, fun-loving, intellectual, non-sexist, young man you married is now, after five years of marriage, a workaholic first and foremost. Even though you work full time too, he seems angry and tired most of the time, and will no longer participate in household tasks—let alone spend much time with the kids. ("It's the wife's job," he says, using words that would never have passed his lips a few years back.) When you call the changes to his attention, his response is: "You're lucky I don't gamble or drink like Johnson down the street does. Don't I bring home my pay every week? And I'm not even having an affair. I work hard to give you and the family a good standard of living and all you do is nag and fuss. I'm fed up!" And you think, "Is this the person I was crazy about a few years ago?"

What happened? From all indications every couple above was (once upon a time) in love—yet each marriage is a loser. Each couple would have benefited greatly from a pre-marriage decision to take the time and energy to sort out a lot of issues, questions, conflicts, and problems that will eventually surface during just about any marriage. (For some of the issues and problems you should discuss with each other, please see Chapter Four.) And yes. You can begin this process before either of you walks down the aisle.

Before asking the questions and discussing the issues with your partner, however, you need to have an effective way of communicating. In fact, an effective communication model is perhaps the most important element in secure and lasting marriages. Start using this method now with friends, lovers, and parents. Again, it isn't anything fancy—but it can make all the difference in assessing your relationship's potential. Good communication starts with using "I" messages. Let me give you some examples to show the difference between harmful communication (using "you" messages) and good communication (using non-combative, non-threatening "I" messages).

Instead of telling your partner,

> If I've told you once, I've told you a hundred times that you should be on time when we're meeting someone for dinner.

Try saying,

> It's really embarrassing to me when I have to make excuses for you not coming on time for dinner. I know you don't do it deliberately. Would you like me to call you at the office to remind you? I'd appreciate your cooperation.

Instead of saying,

> If you really loved me you would remember to take out the garbage.

Try saying,

> It upsets me when I have to remind you to take the garbage out. It's a dumb thing to fuss about I know, especially since you agreed it was your job, but do you think we could work out a solution? Should I leave you a note or . . .

Instead of complaining,

> If you cared for me, you wouldn't go fishing with your cronies.

Try saying,

> I know how much you enjoy your fishing trips but with my schedule, the weekends are the only time we get to spend time together. Is there some compromise I can work out with you?

Instead of saying,

> If you really loved me, you wouldn't go on about the troubles you've had at work just when I get home exhausted from my job.

Try saying,

> Honey, I know how difficult it is to work all day. I want to talk about it, but I find I can't be very helpful when we discuss it when I've just gotten home. I'd really appreciate it if we could set another time to talk.

Instead of verbally attacking your partner, saying,

> If you had even the least bit of consideration for me you wouldn't hang out with that silly friend of yours, Leslie. You know I can't stand Leslie.

Say:

> Darling, I realize that we have different opinions about some of our friends. I would be more comfortable if I didn't know about the time you spend with Leslie.

If your partner says, "You seem upset," instead of saying,

> No, I'm not. Why do you always want to start arguments?

Say:

> I guess there must be something wrong, because I'm not feeling upset. What do you think is happening?

In each of the examples, the latter approach represents the

positive communication skills that healthy relationships develop. Now is a good time for you to practice these "I" messages. It won't be easy, but it's one of the best preparations for a successful marriage. "I" messages encourage the art of compromise and represent the best way to avoid speaking in attacking, hurtful, blaming ways.

Here are a few other guidelines to keep in mind.

Avoid statements such as,

"You'll never amount to anything . . .",
"You're just plain rotten . . .",
"You hate me/I hate you . . ."
"You always/never . . ."

Why? These statements—and all of their possible variations—tend to polarize a conversation . . . and, by extension, your relationship. They leave your partner with little or no room to respond maturely, as an equal. Once you find a more accessible way to state the same points you feel strongly about, you'll be on the way to a better level of communication.

What is this leading up to? The sooner you learn how to negotiate your relationship's (inevitable) conflicts, the better off you'll be. Whether you like it or not, there will be fights in marriage. And this should not worry anyone. Dr. George Bach, author of *The Intimate Enemy*, sees occasional, intense, angry exchanges as indications of genuine involvement and caring. The trick is to learn how to fight in a non-hurtful way. Messages filled with venomous asides and ominous threats are the first danger signs in a disintegrating relationship.

Here are some of Dr. Bach's rules for fair fighting:

State a specific source of dissatisfaction, without sitting in judgment of the person's whole character.

Do not betray a partner's trust by bringing up vulnerabilities he or she has shared with you.

When a person passes on a gripe, feed it back to him/her as accurately as possible. This encourages listening, rather than waiting for one's turn to talk.

Do not make assumptions about the other person's thoughts, feelings, or motives.

Do not correct a partner's statement about his or her feelings. What he or she feels is his or her reality.

Don't complain for the sake of complaining. Ask for a reasonable change that will relieve the gripe.

Never put restrictive, limiting labels on a partner: child, drunk, neurotic.

I might add that once you do get involved in an argument, saying "It's all my fault" won't help resolve anything. Nor will "It's all your fault; you must be dense not to get what I'm saying," rather than "I'm sorry you feel this way."

"I" messages and fair fights are good things to know about before going into a marriage. But suppose it's after you get married that you fall into the pattern of making hateful statements, fighting unfairly and moving toward a breakup?

Rule Number One is, talk to each other. If you are unsuccessful, try marriage counseling or a marriage encounter group. Don't assume the problem will go away. There is no substitute for finding out "what troubles you about me," and "what troubles me about you."

Try experimenting with a few changes. Agree that you won't (or will) do this or that for a month without complaining and see how it goes. Also, experiment with a radical technique called being nice to each other—even if it's fake. You'd be surprised what a couple of months of old-fashioned politeness can do to a troubled relationship. See what happens when you follow the old rule about not saying anything at all if you can't say something nice.

This approach may sound phony, but it isn't at all. It will give you the breathing space and the energy to consider whether the troubled situation is worth fighting for.

If you're feeling particularly adventurous after a few weeks of this, you might even consider forgiveness. Try reading *Forgive and Forget—Healing the Hurts We Don't Deserve*, by Lewis B. Smedes (Pocket Books, 1984). And after forgiveness, you might be ready to consider Gerald G. Jamplosky's approach in his excellent book, *Love Is Letting Go of Fear* (Bantam Books, 1981). You might still be afraid to take another chance or even make the commitment to the marriage that has been lacking all along. Do remember, however, that until you're willing to risk getting hurt, there's no point in even trying to make the commitment. Every meaningful interaction involves risk.

Of course, there are many more reasons behind failed marriages, including money problems, the birth of a handicapped child, interfering in-laws, marrying too young, or resentment of the spouse over an early problem in the relationship (such as an unwanted pregnancy that "forced" marriage). However, the basic communication rules apply to everyone, regardless of the accompanying circumstances. Learn the rules before you get married.

I suspect you are wondering why I don't mention affairs as a factor in marital breakup. My experience has been that an affair is a symptom of an already "broken" marriage. In fact, an affair by itself rarely breaks up a marriage, and can sometimes initiate new attempts at communication. What the crisis of a revealed affair does is present the couple with the opportunity to decide whether to try again or to call it quits and get a divorce.

We have looked, so far, at the various reasons marriages break up. To conclude this chapter, though, let's look at positive aspects. It's at least as important to do this as to forecast the risks. After all, you don't want a relationship that "doesn't fail," you want one that succeeds in challenging and enriching both partners.

What should a good marriage have?

We'll address the question in detail later in the book, but a few comments are appropriate here. Good marriages invariably involve compromises. The passionate, all-encompassing period of attraction in marriage usually lasts only a few months. Unrealistic expectations and   Hollywood -inspired notions of marriages quickly dissolve with the dependable, daily advance of one's everyday life. Disappointment sets in quickly.

What keeps the best marriages going is commitment to the other person in the relationship. Commitment becomes the key issue after a rational decision to marry.

No marriage really works unless both partners are committed to each other's growth, and unless, as M. Scott Peck has suggested in his excellent book, *The Road Less Travelea*, a person makes a commitment to be loving whether or not a reciprocal loving feeling is present. In effect, this commitment says, "Yes, there will be anger and fights. And yes, we'll try to work out a system of resolving arguments. I will stay with you. I'll be patient, and I will love you even when you are not lovable. I hope you will do the same for me."

Chapter Four:
One on One—Questions,
Issues, and Problems

MANY COUPLES DAYDREAM a great deal about all the wonderful things they'd like to see happen once they get married. There's nothing wrong with that; it's certainly enjoyable. But, in addition to the daydreaming, I'd urge you to take the time to consider some "real-life" questions.

It's very important to sort out the potential issues, questions, and conflicts you and your partner may bring to the relationship. In this chapter, we'll try to examine what sorts of questions you should be asking once you feel confident that you've entered into a mature relationship—one you'd like to see grow into something special.

The very act of composing a list of "questions you should ask" is something of an exercise in optimism. After all, no two relationships are alike, and no one can anticipate all the potential challenges and decisions a couple will face. Nevertheless, it's essential to make the effort. If you don't pose the applicable "what if" questions (and you should certainly feel free to add your own questions to my list), you may be rudely awakened later on in your relationship when you and your partner disagree violently over something that should have been discussed before you decided to marry.

Marriage

While the main thrust of this book addresses the challenges facing those attempting to build a lasting love relationship, the questions I'll be posing in this chapter are, for the most part, of greatest relevance to those couples who are seriously considering getting married. With that in mind, it's probably a good idea to discuss the institution of marriage.

There are, of course, many different kinds of marriages. There are marriages of convenience, which feature little long-term passion or intimacy; there are marriages of desperation, in which one or both of the partners may have to confront significant self-esteem problems; there are "old fashioned" marriages, with rigidly defined gender roles; and there are what I call the "best-case" marriages, those which offer an exciting balance of intimacy, passion, and commitment. My suggestions in this chapter are directed toward those couples in a mature relationship who feel that the last option is the one they'd like to pursue as a marital objective. Furthermore, I'm assuming that the relationship is more or less egalitarian in nature.

Let me explain what I mean by that. An egalitarian relationship does not require that the wife be prohibited from staying at home and taking care of the children, and forced instead to "find a real job." (Child care and the domestic duties associated with it are easily equivalent to at least one full time job and probably more, as anyone who's tried it can tell you.) Furthermore, an egalitarian relationship doesn't demand that the man automatically forego the role of "breadwinner," nor does it dictate that a woman can't cook and prepare all the meals if this arrangement is based on mutual agreement.

What an egalitarian relationship does demand is a commitment to equal opportunities in decision making, specifically including choices related to career, childrearing, and lifestyle questions. It's in this context that the strongest marriages address important issues, and it's to couples who want to build such marriages that the following points are addressed.

The Questions

Before you ask your partner any of the following questions, it might be a good idea to discuss the important topics of honesty and risk-taking in your relationship. A number of the issues addressed below are considered sensitive by many people. If your partner is prepared for such questions, you're more likely to have a productive discussion.

Careers

(If both couples work:) Does it matter who earns the most?

(If both couples work:) What if one of us is offered a new job at significantly higher levels of pay and responsibility—in a different part of the country? What is my reaction if it's you? What is your reaction if it's me?

What if one of us wants to pursue further education or get a higher degree?

What if one of us wants to start a new business?

What about retirement plans?

Family

Do we want children? If so, when and how many?

Will we share in caring for the baby, including diaper changes?

Does either of us have strong feelings about how a child should or should not be raised? If so, what are they? If not, how should we address the issue?

Finances

Will we have separate or joint bank accounts?

Will we need life insurance? If so, how much?

Is a prenuptial agreement appropriate? How do you feel about such agreements?

Should we save as much of our income as we can, or try to live as well as possible on what we make now? If we decide to save, what do we hope to do with the money?

What do you think about borrowing money? Credit cards?

Assuming that we have the choice on a purchase of a major appliance (say, a refrigerator) should we give most serious consideration to a top-of-the-line model or something that's on sale? Why?

Of the two of us, who is the biggest spender? How does the other partner feel about this?

Is it important to either of us to purchase an item primarily because a neighbor or other acquaintance has a similar item?

Living Arrangements

Where will we live once we get married?

Does either of us have strong feelings about furniture, design, or floor plans in our living space?

How will we allocate household tasks? Does either of us have strong likes or dislikes about particular tasks?

Personal

How do we usually handle disagreements?

How much of our past have we shared with each other up to this point? Is it necessary to share everything?

With whose parents do we anticipate spending most of our "in-law" time, such as holidays and family gatherings? Will we attempt to "split" this time? How will we handle any problems that may arise in this area? Does either of us feel we must kowtow to future in-laws? What happens if we tire of doing so?*

---

* If in-laws try to interfere, or unduly influence your marriage, it's best to work out some kind of specific compromise with your spouse. You might reach an agreement along the following lines: "We'll go to your folks' place for Thanksgiving and I'll listen to their harangues politely, but without commitments to change things about which I simply disagree. On Christmas Day, we'll go to my folks' house, and then *you* can play sweetness and light without having to pay attention to any of the snide remarks they make about your cooking." Again, it's okay under certain circumstances to fake it!

What level of support do our parents anticipate for their old age?

How important is religion in our life together?

Do we have to be together all the time? Can we have separate interests? What about occasional separate vacations?

In addition to our mutual acquaintances, can we have friends whom the other partner does not know or spend time with? What if one of us has a friend the other genuinely dislikes?

How do we feel about pets? Do either of us have strong negative reactions or allergies to certain animals?

How should we spend our leisure time together? Are we willing to compromise on this issue if there is a disagreement?

If either of us does something the other person doesn't like, can we . . .

a) agree not to confront each other about it in public, and discuss it in an appropriate private setting?

b) address the issue in a polite manner?

c) listen to the other person's reaction to the criticism objectively?

Assume that one of us finds someone else attractive, appealing, or interesting. Is it all right to say so? Or would you prefer that I kept it to myself? Would I prefer that you do the same?

How would either of us feel if there were some irritating character trait or behavior which the other person was unwilling or unable to change?

Are there things either of us finds unappealing about the other person? What have we avoided saying to keep from hurting the other person's feelings? Are there "ticking bombs" that may eventually explode in any of the following areas?

Quirks

Poor hygiene or bad breath

Little or no sense of humor

Personal mannerisms

Clothes selection or general appearance

Behavior in front of in-laws or friends

Compulsive behavior

Suppose one of us is infertile. Would we remain childless? Divorce? Adopt a child? If adoption is our response, do we have any preconditions (for instance, that the child be of a certain race or sex)? Would we explore other "fertility options"?

Suppose (God forbid) we have a child who is born severely handicapped. How would we respond? What would the implications of caring for such a child be in relation to our other life objectives?

If one of us wants something from the relationship and doesn't get it, can the topic be raised diplomatically, and not in a confrontational manner? If the other partner feels as though he or she is being attacked in such situations, how will we keep communication lines open?

How willing are we to give up something that may be important to the other person in order to make a realistic compromise?

If one of us is not in the mood to have sex when the other partner suggests it, will we be able to remember that we still both care about and love each other?

What do we hope our life together will be like five years from now? Ten years from now?

(Regardless of age:) When I grow up, I'd like to be a _____. What would you like to be when you grow up?

What do you least like about yourself? What do I least like about myself? Can we work out a system that will allow each of us (discreetly) to tell the other person when he or she is engaging in activities we agree need improvement?

We feel good about the relationship now, but what if one of us, someday, feels the urge to have an affair? What is the difference between fantasizing about an affair and actually engaging in one? What about flirting with others — do we consider it "harmless"? If one of us were to genuinely desire to have an affair, are our communication skills strong enough to discuss a potential crisis openly? Would we see a marriage counselor? Most important, do we trust each other not to let the marriage disintegrate by perpetuating a dishonest approach to our relationship?

Of course, over the years, there are hundreds of other issues that will arise in a marriage. But the points addressed above represent a healthy start in sorting out problems and potential trouble spots. Asking (and honestly answering) questions like the ones posed in this chapter will strengthen your relationship and encourage both partners to develop mature communication skills.

Men and Women, Women and Men

Issues like the ones I've outlined here are important to address *before* the marriage because of the potentially disastrous effects of learning, after the honeymoon, that one's spouse has rigid expectations in areas that were misinterpreted (or simply not discussed) early in the relationship. Many of the commonest misunderstandings are gender-based. Research into the causes of modern marriage problems has consistently shown that there are significant differences in the ways men and women are socialized to accept marital roles. No matter how strongly you feel about your relationship, you should know about these general tendencies on the part of each sex before you get married.

For instance, most women tend to view intimacy as a shared commitment to address important issues and problems—as a couple. Men, by contrast, often feel they've fulfilled their obligations once they've "done their share" (e.g., performed specific, predetermined chores, brought home a paycheck according to schedule, or taken the next "turn" putting the children to bed).

Another point of departure: conflict resolution. While women typically view the discussion of differences as a way to get closer to their partners, men generally seek to avoid confrontations and blowups.

In addition, many wives build stronger relationships with their parents after marriage, while husbands tend, on the whole, to become more distant with theirs. (It's not uncommon to see the *wife* making an effort to maintain contact with her mother- and/or father-in-law once the husband has "detached.")

And while men often put a great deal of energy and caring into the "courtship" period before a marriage, after the honeymoon their general tendency is to give higher priority to work, friends, and outside interests. In extreme cases, the wife may eventually feel displaced or even abandoned.

Of course, there are no hard-and-fast rules in this area. Though men and women may tend to take different approaches to certain life experiences, each individual man and woman in each individual marriage remains (thank goodness) a unique person blessed with the gifts of discretion and choice. The generalizations are helpful only in two very specific areas: setting guidelines and agreements before the marriage, so that neither partner is taken by surprise later on; and preparing for your relationship's growth over time.

Pre-Marriage Activities

Once you've asked and answered the questions that will have most relevance to your life as a couple, what do you do next?

First, you should evaluate your partner's (and your own) answers objectively. With any luck, you'll have a better idea of who your potential mate really is, what his or her strong points are, where there are weaknesses (as there are with any human being), and how well the two of you communicate. How do you feel about what you've learned?

You probably shouldn't depend on your ability to "reform" your partner during the marriage. It's usually futile to try to change your partner to conform to some ideal; you are marrying the person you are marrying, for better or for worse, and once you are married you'll need to develop a certain amount of tolerance and a good sense of humor . . . because, in the end, you'll have to accept your partner "as is." Though the approach may seem a little fatalistic, it accurately reflects the conditions of the vast majority of marriages, even the most successful ones. (Again, nothing is impossible; however, a total change in your partner's personality is unlikely.)

Still feel you need more information? I've listed below a number of activities that you and your partner can try together before you make a final decision to get married. Try the ones that seem most appealing to you as a couple. Once you've completed the activity, review your experiences together. Were you comfortable together? When was there tension? How do each of you feel about your communication skills as a couple? Evaluating the activities honestly will give you a good idea of what you might expect over the course of your marriage.

Except for the last two, each of the following activities will help virtually any couple test their compatibility, regardless of whether or not an intimate sexual relationship exists.

Go on a two-week vacation, all by yourselves, to a place where you can't easily be reached. Don't visit any friends or relatives. See how well you manage.

Agree to babysit for friends or relatives for one full weekend or longer. (Try to arrange caring for children under the age of ten.)

Spend a day "window shopping" for a (hypothetical, if necessary) house or apartment full of furniture; find out where you agree and disagree on matters of taste in furnishings.

Spend two whole days in each other's company without watching any television. Each partner should plan one full day's worth of activities.

Pick a favorite relative from each partner's family to visit together.

Make a list of your traits. Each person should write what he or she considers to be the five most and five least attractive qualities of both partners. Compare notes and discuss why the lists don't agree. (They won't.)

Do a mitzvah together. (You might decide, for instance, to work with disadvantaged children one night a week.)

Spend an entire afternoon at an art or natural history museum together.

Have dinner at an "ethnic" restaurant neither of you has tried before.

Find a beautiful park, meadow, or other peaceful surrounding. Take a long walk together.

Attend and participate in three or four of *either* of the following:

a) synagogue or church services.

b) community, political, or conservation group meetings.

For sexually active partners: *

Vary your sexual methods. Try experimenting with new positions, settings, and times for lovemaking. If you need ideas, consult the bibliography of this book, which includes references for a number of the better sex manuals. (I strongly recommend that you use a reliable contraceptive system, preferably one that incorporates a condom.)

Schedule separate professional massages, and make mental note of the techniques used. Then, one day, give each other massages that take advantage of all you've learned. (You might do this at a time when you'd normally make love. It doesn't matter whether the massages are sexually stimulating or not.) I'm not suggesting that it will take only one session for you to become a professional masseur—luckily, you don't have to be a professional to give an enjoyable massage.

---

* It's interesting to note that whether or not you decide to live together or become sexually intimate before marriage seems not to be a crucial factor with regard to whether the marriage will succeed or not. Current American data is inconclusive. Large scale Canadian studies (reported by psychologist James M. White in *Psychology Today,* March 1988) suggested that cohabitators were somewhat more likely than others to stay married.

Chapter Five:
People You Shouldn't Marry

LET'S FACE THE facts. There are some people you'd be absolutely *nuts* to marry. Some relationships simply cause more pain than joy, and are, frankly, unlikely to work out well for either partner.

As we all know, many marriages these days end in failure. There's no reason you should make the statistics more depressing than they already are by entering into a marriage that's unlikely to succeed. Even if your own situation doesn't quite fall into the category of "accident waiting to happen," you should know that there are a great many relationships that fall into a kind of grey area. These are relationships in which it's probably not a bad idea to get married eventually, though the partners should think long and hard about what they want before making a final decision.

If you are involved with someone and the topic of getting married is either raised or likely to be raised, I suggest you use the following guidelines. They may help you avoid a serious mistake: committing yourself to a destructive, exhausting, unhealthy, or just plain unhappy marriage.

The "Dont's"

Don't marry . . . an addict.* And be sure to bear in mind that people can be addicted to things other than drugs. If your partner is an alcoholic, a drug abuser, a child molester, a womanizer, a compulsive gambler, or exhibits self-destructive dependent behavior in any other area, do not offer to share in the dependency by getting married; neither of you will be happier for it.

You must make every effort to be honest with yourself about your partner. If your partner's situation has reached a point of genuine addiction—meaning that his or her behavior is compulsive, not voluntary—you're asking for trouble by getting married. Addicts will give their addiction priority over everything else in life, including health, family, friends, and, yes, you. To make matters worse, addicts lie a lot. They also betray friends and family routinely, rarely keep promises, are big on denial, blame others (especially spouses) for their problems, and have a remarkable fondness for instant gratification over just about anything else in life.

However attractive, good-natured, or reasonable addicts seem, they eventually turn out to be con artists. To marry one is to make matters worse.

If you love an addict, don't offer to get married. A person who marries an addict becomes a co-dependent who *facilitates* the disease's progression and *enhances* its harmful effects. Virtually all studies in this area indicate that your *independence* is more helpful to the addict than your co-dependence!

---

*I am referring here only to someone who is in the so-called "disease" stage, not to addicts who are recovered or recovering. With all addicts, however, one must bear in mind that relapse is a genuine possibility, even after long periods of convalescence. In any case, it's usually best to decide against marrying someone in this category who hasn't demonstrated at least a year or so of "sobriety."

You can help the addict most by trying to convince him or her to seek treatment. Most (but not all) addicts can gain a lot through participating in a program that uses the Alcoholics Anonymous model. Ask your rabbi, clergyman, or local hotline service for suggestions on where to go for more information.

Don't marry. . . anyone who is violent towards you or abuses you emotionally. Husband or wife, young or old, there's no excuse for emotional or physical abuse of one's spouse. (And to my way of thinking, a "battered spouse" is one who undergoes *any* abusive or recurrent attacks, whether verbal or physical.)

It's sad but true that most battered wives started out as battered girlfriends. That's why it's so important to keep in mind that violence is the *opposite* of mature love. Period.

If you are involved in a violent relationship, you should know that aggressive and abusive behavior is *always* a sign of despair, distress, loneliness, neurosis, and feelings of inferiority. As if that weren't enough, violence sometimes is a symptom of (literally) murderous criminal potential.

Why do people stay in violent relationships? The answer is complex. Many women (and a surprising number of men), when asked, "Why do you stay with someone who only seems to want to hurt you?", will answer, "I love him (her)." It's more likely that the person feels unloved by anyone, has feelings of powerlessness and hopelessness, and holds a strong belief that there are simply no other options.

Many battered women reveal in therapy that they were abused as children, often while being lectured by a parent, along the lines of, "I'm doing this for your own good, because I love you." Further evidence suggests that the violence in relationships may run in cycles; many men who beat their wives and girlfriends were themselves abused children.

If you're ever attacked physically by the person who claims to love you, draw the line then and there. My advice is to be prepared to forgive, but with a warning. Tell your partner flatly that if the violence ever makes a return appearance, you're leaving, and that's it. Then stick to your word. You might be willing to listen to the promises to atone—once. After that, it's time to move on, conceivably to one of the available shelters for battered spouses, and perhaps to therapy (which is often the remedy for the violent spouse, as well). Though it may be difficult and frightening to take the first step, the sad fact is that remaining in a violent relationship is a losing proposition.

Don't "marry" . . . someone who's already married. In other words, don't count on a married person divorcing his or her spouse and then marrying you.

I'm not going to tell you that it's impossible to form a lifelong relationship with someone who's already committed. But I can tell you that the odds aren't very encouraging. In the vast majority of cases, the "secondary" relationship never works out. Most of the men and women who have affairs with married people . . . have affairs with married people. And that's it. The encounters are just interludes, flings—not serious relationships.

Most people don't give up their marriages over affairs. (Of course, it's another matter if your lover is already separated and waiting for a divorce to be finalized.) But the temptation for many still exists to try to make something out of what will, eventually probably be nothing.

I'm often asked if there is any reliable way to tell if the married lover (usually a man) is "really serious." In my view, the best way to estimate the odds of such a relationship working out is to be brutally honest and gauge the time preference of the married partner. If he or she is in the process of leaving a dying relationship, and still tends to spend weekends away from you, leaving time only for "brief encounters," it's not an encouraging signal.

People who play games make a lot of mistakes. They tell lies, they make promises they can't keep, they keep a lot of secrets, they keep you waiting on street corners. People who aren't "serious" are preoccupied with themselves; they forget important occasions in your life and can't seem to remember things that should be important to both of you.

Other "Risk Groups"

Apart from the broader guidelines I've set out above, you'll want to consider whether you or your partner fall into certain "high risk" categories, groups that are (generally) more likely to end up divorcing. Many marriages end unhappily, not because the spouses are inherently bad people, but simply because they neglected, before committing to marriage, to examine carefully the many factors that influence relationships over time.

Don't marry. . .

. . . if both partners are still young. Marriages between two partners who are under twenty-one are more likely than not to end in divorce or separation.

. . . if you feel you have a bad relationship with either of your parents, and your prospective spouse seems to you to be someone "just like" that parent.

. . . if the partners consistently seem to have difficulty accepting each other's ideas, fight most of the time, or simply don't appear to understand each other.

. . . if conversations frequently contain any of the following phrases:

"Do you really love me?" "Are you sure it's me you love?" "I wish you were more like . . ." "You have to give up *those* friends. We can only have mutual friends now." "I can't stand it when you spend time alone reading (pursuing a hobby) (meditating) (whatever). You should spend every minute you can with me."

. . . if your decision to get married has been heavily influenced by either partner's parents. Many people, seduced by the acceptance, flattery, wealth, or even cooking of a potential in-law, find themselves at the altar promising to spend their lives with someone for whom they don't have any genuine feelings.

. . . if your partner has traits you abhor (such as a violent temper or poor grooming habits), yet you find yourself unable to raise the issue for fear of offending.

. . . if you find yourself being too anxious to please a partner who gives little in return, or you feel he or she makes consistently selfish demands and rarely considers your welfare.

. . . if, after extensive discussion, you're still unable to agree on where you're going to live or under what circumstances (i.e., career changes or new income opportunities elsewhere) you would move in the future.

. . . if your values regarding material goods are radically different. Couples often have major conflicts when they realize, after getting married, that one spouse prefers a modest standard of living, while the other insists on lavish surroundings and a steady ascent up the ladder of success.

. . . if either partner is desperate to marry as soon as possible. If only for your own sake, don't marry anyone out of panic or pressure from another person. No matter who's applying the pressure, and no matter what the reason (pregnancy, the need to leave home, a ticking biological clock, the desire to fit in with "all your friends" who are married, loneliness, fear of independence, or any of the other possibilities), it is *always* best to delay a decision to get married if any given factor has convinced you that you "must" walk down the altar immediately. (In addition, you should be alert if your partner becomes so preoccupied with wedding plans that you feel neglected—as though it's not happening to you.)

For further suggestions on the difficult job of establishing whether or not your relationship can support a lifetime commitment, consult the bibliography at the end of this book. It will supply you with the titles of some excellent books in the field. Don't be put off by a book's addressing itself to women if you're a man, or vice-versa; I particularly recommend those books that allow the reader to get a glimpse of how the opposite sex views the problems and issues surrounding love, commitment, and relationships.

On The Fence

While there are many people you shouldn't marry, there's a special category of people about whom it's particularly hard to make a judgment one way or the other: the fence-sitters.

These are the on-again, off-again people who postpone engagements or constantly hedge on the subject of getting married; they're afraid of making a commitment. Many reasons may underlie this fear.

A lot of people look for perfection in a relationship—and nobody's perfect. Some "fence-sitters" are afraid of making a mistake in choosing a mate, always convinced that "somebody better" is out there waiting to be discovered. Others are reluctant to lose their independence or say goodbye to the freedom and good times they've known. Still others are fearful of responsibility, and anticipate the worst in everything, asking themselves how they'll cope with all the crises that loom in the future: "What if I lose my job? What if we can't pay the mortgage? What if our child is born retarded?"

Then there are those who always seem to be preoccupied with what others might think, and use others' opinions as an excuse to delay a decision. Their own judgment or evaluations never carry as much weight as those of the outside world: "He's not handsome enough for my crowd." "My parents aren't doing cartwheels over her, that's for sure." "Marrying him might make me happy, but as far as prestige goes, it wouldn't be much of a catch compared to what my sister ended up with."

All of this puts the "fence-sitter's" partner in a difficult situation. When are the indecisive person's objections legitimate, and when are they simply shields against a choice? Does the inability to come to a decision indicate that there's a likelihood of future problems in the potential marriage? What do you do if you're really in love with a "fence-sitter," one you feel strongly about marrying?

The only way out of the ambivalence may be to force a decision. Once you've made every effort to talk through all the issues and problems surrounding your relationship, set a deadline for an answer one way or the other. While this may well lead to an emotionally charged situation, remember that you won't be asking for anything unreasonable — just a final, authoritative answer to a big question so you can get on with your life.

And keep in mind that there's not necessarily any reason for you to end either the friendship or the love relationship if the answer is "no." Though you may need to take some time on your own, or have genuine feelings of disappointment to deal with, there's no reason to burn bridges. Most people can use all the friends they can get. On the other hand, of course, ending the relationship might just be the very best thing that could happen to you. In any event, make the decision in terms of what's best for you.

Other Judgment Calls

Like the "fence-sitter," there are a number of other categories of people who deserve close scrutiny before you decide to spend your life with them. You should consider marrying, but be very careful about. . .

A divorced person. Perhaps as many as half of all previously divorced people will divorce again. Unfortunately, when it comes to failed marriages, there is a definite tendency to make the same mistake more than once; many divorced people don't establish accurately enough why their previous marriages didn't work out.

If you are considering marrying a person who's had a divorce, try to discuss the previous marriage's problems in some detail. Ask your partner why he or she feels that this time around will be different—and what elements of the relationship will be the same.

If your partner's response is something along the lines of "I don't want to talk about it," watch out. You're being shown a very clear danger signal, and you should proceed with utmost caution.

Before marrying a divorced person, make sure that all agreements with the ex-spouse are in writing and that you have reviewed these agreements carefully. You wouldn't believe the disasters you can find yourself walking into when there are significant unresolved conflicts between a divorced couple, especially conflicts regarding children.

Though they're certainly not the best way to begin a marriage, fights between your partner and his or her former spouse may well come with the territory, and you should be aware of any serious disagreements before you decide to get married. Whatever else you do, discuss the issue openly and settle on a strategy that will help you to cope with such conflicts. My advice is to stay above the fray. If you don't remain polite, non-threatening, and calm, you'll probably make matters worse. If at all possible, stay away from trials and court proceedings. (Obviously, marrying a divorced person with children presents many challenges. I'll deal with the thorny issue of making a healthy adjustment to an "adopted family" in more detail later on in this book.)

A widow or widower. If the previous marriage was relatively good, then your chances for success in marrying a widow or widower are probably better than if you were marrying a divorced person. However, you should be prepared for the possibility that your partner will eventually make some unfavorable comparisons between you and his or her previous spouse. A deceased spouse may be idealized by the survivor. There may even be some episodes of fantasy and denial.

Your goal will be to remind your mate gently that everyone is unique, and that it is unrealistic and unfair for him or her to expect to re-enter the previous marriage. This relationship should represent a new experience, a new opportunity, a chance to begin again. If you feel that regular, unflattering comparisons with someone you'll never be able to surpass are going to be a permanent component of the marriage, think seriously about how happy you will be in such a situation.

Someone who is more than ten years older or younger than you are. There's not necessarily any serious problem here, but it's a good idea for both of you to be aware of the long-term age barriers that may present themselves (i.e., "When he's fifty, I'll be thirty-five") and to be sure of each other's true motivations.

Are there factors at work that neither person has admitted (for instance, money or status)? Does the relationship encourage good communication? If there are "mothering" or "fathering" tendencies, how do you feel about this?

Someone who has a serious handicap. Again, it's a good idea to examine your motivations. In a mature relationship, as long as considerations of financial gain, for instance, or pity don't enter into the picture, and as long as all the sensitive issues relating to topics like sexuality and long-term care have been addressed openly, there's probably a good chance for success.

Someone who is bisexual or homosexual. Many homosexuals, and perhaps a majority of bisexuals, get married. If the thousands of enthusiastic letters received by Ann Landers upon addressing the issue in a recent column are any indication, many such marriages are successful.

The key here, as you might imagine, is honesty. Obviously, each partner must disclose the relevant facts about his or her sexuality, and there must be clear agreements regarding what constitutes acceptable behavior. It's surprising to many people, but nevertheless true, that there can be very good marriages that don't feature a superlative sex life as their central element.

Marriages to homosexuals usually fail when honesty is lacking, and often in the context of the "secret" being discovered in explosive circumstances—in much the same way that a heterosexual marriage may self-destruct if one partner engages in a secret long-term affair and is "caught."

(These days, unfortunately, no one should consider marriage to a homosexual or a bisexual—or, for that matter, any other risk group member—without asking the partner to take a test which screens for the HIV virus responsible for AIDS.)

Someone with a different religious background. Interfaith marriages are more common now than they once were, but the fact remains that, even if each partner is non-affiliated and non-practicing, such couples probably stand a greater chance of divorcing than couples who are of the same religion.

When people from different religious backgrounds first announce that they intend to marry, tensions are often high; frequently, parents object to the marriage. However, in the end, the decision to marry is usually accepted by all parties.

It's later on that most of the most significant problems emerge. What religion will the children practice? How should the couple deal with relatives and friends still very committed to their own religion? What about the celebration of holidays? Often, the "compromises" attempted bring little comfort. (Many Jews, for instance, frown on couples who celebrate both Christmas and Hanukkah.)

In my view, it's easier to marry someone from your own background. Nevertheless, marrying a person you love is infinitely preferable to marrying someone you don't, religion or no religion. I encourage interfaith couples to discuss all the relevant issues fully and openly, to consider seriously the option of formal conversion (probably to the minority religion), and to be prepared for ongoing examination of the challenges inherent to such marriages.

Chapter Six:
Letting Go

IF THE PAIN of being with the person you love far outweighs the joy you share . . .

If your love is more of a burden than a pleasure . . .

If you feel desperate or lonely when you are with your partner, but closer to him or her, somehow, when you're apart. . .

If you're terrified at the idea of not finding someone else. . .

If your partner's behavior overpowers you and brings you to a point of despair and loss of dignity . . .

Then it's time to let go of your relationship.

Easier Said Than Done

Extricating oneself from a destructive or painful relationship is one of the most difficult tasks we can face in life. And it's a lot easier to talk about it than it is to do it. But when it must be done, it must be done.

In this chapter, we'll take a look at some of the problems facing people in difficult love relationships, and examine some of the options available that will eventually allow you to move on.

A victimized or unsatisfied partner may have been

experiencing frustration, anger, and pain for years—without ever developing the tools necessary to let go. What stands in the way? There are many possible reasons, and many defenses offered in hopes of maintaining the status quo.

"I love him (her)." (Probably. But there's also a very good chance that the overriding characteristic of the relationship is an inability to support mutual, mature love and affection.)

"My lover has threatened to commit suicide." (Though you can certainly have sympathy for someone undergoing an emotional crisis, this is still no reason to stay in a bad relationship. If you are really worried, be sure that your partner's parents and/or friends know about your feelings. Delay conveying your intentions to leave—at least until you can be sure he or she is in a safe place, such as with family.)

"It will break his (her) heart." (People get over pain and suffering a lot faster when you deal with them honestly, rather than continuing to foster an environment that doesn't represent reality. You have genuine needs. Express them. Staying in a bad relationship will do neither of you any good in the long run.)

"At least this way I'll be financially secure." (Are you sure about that? Are you sure your partner isn't in fact draining you for all you're worth? Are you sure your only option is to continue along the same path, even though it's making you miserable? Have you honestly examined other resources, such as employment and training programs or support groups?)

"I'm frightened; if I leave, I'll probably be lonely for the rest of my life." (If you'll make the effort to be honest with yourself, you'll probably recognize that you're very lonely right now. And you're likely to get more lonely: the longer you live with someone you don't like – or worse, someone you hate – the lonelier you'll be.)

What You Can Expect

How do you let go of a destructive relationship and get on with your life?

First, take time out to think. Review what you feel is least satisfying or most threatening about the relationship. Then become very specific.

Determine the two or three aspects of your life with your partner that are most painful or difficult for you to tolerate. (If there are more than three, select the three most important.) Write them down if it helps.

In private, take the time to go over the items in detail. Memorize them, so that it will not be possible for you to forget what you want to talk about.

Then, when you feel confident that you've isolated exactly what makes the relationship difficult for you, take time to sit down and talk it out. Be attentive to the setting you choose, to timing, and to your partner's frame of mind. If you've decided to leave because your lover drinks too much, it's not a good idea to announce your departure when he or she has come home at two in the morning dead drunk.

Tell your partner that you now find it too difficult and too stressful to continue the relationship unless there is rapid and noticeable improvement in certain areas. Then outline the problems you identified on your own earlier.   Do this without assuming a confrontational attitude. It will not help your position to make cruel remarks about your partner's personality or potential. Just tell the truth as you see it.

It will be easier for you if you can anticipate the reactions and be ready to answer them. I've listed a number of possible reactions and responses below.

Why are you doing this to me? I'm doing this for myself.

I can't live without you. I have to be able to live with myself. I can't go on with broken promises, and I can't keep trying to make such a painful relationship work.

I love you and you hate me. Of course I love you; but love isn't enough to keep a relationship going. Being able to trust you counts, too. Being able to know you'll be there for me, that you care enough to try to change (problem), that you want to help me and not just have me help you, all of that counts, as well. Those things matter just as much as love in a relationship, and ours doesn't work because those things aren't there. I have to do this; we aren't good for each other right now.

If you aren't quite certain that the relationship should be terminated, you can take a middle course—outline the problems to your partner, then set a deadline for genuine change (say, one month). If, after that period of time, there has been no improvement, you'll be perfectly justified in telling your partner that your own sanity and dignity demand that you let go. Another option is to "force" counseling—suggesting that this course of action represents your last compromise.

The Aftermath

After you've broken up, don't rush out and try to find another romance. It will take you some time to bounce back emotionally. Your life has undergone a significant change; take as long as necessary to gather all the pieces again and get a good idea of who the new, independent you really is.

Reflect on the experience. What did you learn from it? Consider keeping a notebook of your observations during this crucial period.

Review the ideas in Chapter One and make new efforts to improve yourself, learn new things, and do mitzvahs. In addition, you might put new effort into developing any friendships with others you may have been neglecting. Again, try to concentrate on same-sex friends. Do not pressure yourself to become romantically involved.

You will probably go through periods of unhappiness, loneliness, and pain. This is natural, and should not be misinterpreted as a sign that you "belong" back in the unhealthy relationship. If, after a while, your situation does not improve, try to get counseling or join a support group.

Avoid blaming yourself. No one is ever totally at fault in any failed relationship; virtually every breakup is caused by a complex group of factors, some of which can be traced to one person and some of which can't.

Albert Ellis, in his excellent book, *How To Stubbornly Refuse to Make Yourself Miserable About Anything—Yes, Anything!* offers helpful suggestions in this area. "If you are disappointed," Ellis writes, "and regretful about being rejected by a love partner, you will try to discover why you were abandoned, to win back that person's love, or to attempt to mate with a more suitable partner. But if you are angry at your rejector, you will antagonize him or her and remain an enemy instead of a friend. And if you are depressed about being rejected, you will tend to withdraw completely and see yourself as quite unloveable."

This is a learning time. You are adding to your knowledge of the way things work in human relationships, even during your most difficult moments. Among the things you'll have the chance to learn now is the stark fact that many of the clichés that surround love, the phrases that may ring bitterly in your ears in your relationship's aftermath, are just that—clichés. Opposites do not necessarily attract. Love is not necessarily forever. Love cannot conquer all. Love isn't blind.

Proceed from the assumption that you are a good person, even outside the framework of your relationship. In time, the wounds will heal and the scars will fade.

Interlude:
Taking Stock

NOW IT'S TIME to take a look at yourself.

If you've tried some of the ideas I've outlined earlier in the book, and you feel better about yourself and your relationships with others – great! If, however, you feel that you're struggling, or that noticeable results have been slow in coming, we'll take a look at some of the possible reasons why (and suggest some alternative approaches) in this chapter.

What Could Be Standing in the Way?

There are a number of short-term reasons – and one long-term reason – that people have difficulty doing well in their relationships with others. Here are some of the former:

They have difficulty focusing on the needs of others. (This is where mitzvahs can help!)

They appear boring. (Because they never take the time to acquire passionate specialties or interests.)

They talk too much. (Usually about themselves and the injustices visited on them by the world at large.)

They don't say much to anybody. (They believe they won't have anything interesting to offer in conversation. . . a self-fulfilling prophecy.)

They're overly critical of others, or blame innocent people for things they didn't do. (Never an attractive quality)

They don't keep confidences. (It's hard to get close to someone who has a history of repeating your most intimate secrets to anyone who'll listen.)

They bombard themselves with negative messages. (Like, "All the really good people are married.")

They're angry because other people have hurt them. (Forgiveness? Who wants to offer forgiveness? This crowd wants revenge, and doesn't want to discuss anything else, thank you.)

They're terrified of the prospect of taking a risk. (Meanwhile, they're risking a lifetime acquaintance with loneliness and bitterness by not reaching out to someone.)

The Biggie

So much for the short-term factors. There is a larger problem that underlies virtually every one of the roadblocks I've just described—habitually low self-esteem. We noted earlier Mrs. Roosevelt's observation that no one can make you feel inferior without your consent. Now it's time to address the enduring mystery of exactly why so many people routinely give that consent.

Everybody has *tzuris* (Yiddish for "troubles"), but people who feel inferior seem to have more than their share. Perhaps the heart of the problem rests in the way such people look at themselves.

Who you are and how you feel about yourself are tremendously important factors when it comes to long-term happiness. What messages are you sending out about yourself? What kinds of things have you come to believe about yourself? Do you want to believe those things?

There are, in my view, seven "cardinal sins" that will eventually enable you to convince yourself that you're unattractive, uninteresting, laden with serious character defects, and unable to sustain a mature relationship. And by the time you get done convincing yourself, you know what? You'll probably be right.

One: Constant unfavorable comparisons of yourself to others. Yes. There will always be individuals who appear to be handsomer, richer, luckier, or better educated than you are. Unfortunately, none of them has the privilege of being you. That's their tough luck.

Each of us is unique. Each of us is special. Each person has a particular, vital mission in life, one that no one else can accomplish. One of the most revered Jewish sages, Reb Zusya, is reported to have said on his deathbed, "God will not ask me why I was not like Moses. He will ask me why I wasn't myself."

No matter how beautiful or successful anyone else is, *you have your place and your mission.* We are all unique individuals, destined to serve God (or humanity, if you prefer) in a special way. And if you think fulfilling your mission is a self-centered activity, there are thousands of years of scholarship, philosophy, and theology that point in a different direction; many Hassidic Jews, for instance, believe that the reason the Messiah is delayed is that somewhere, one or more people are not trying hard enough to fulfill the purpose of serving the Almighty.

Two: The belief that you won't amount to much "unless I get married." "Unless someone falls in love with me." "Unless someone needs me." "Unless I make a lot of money." "Unless my parents are satisfied with my achievements."

The fact is, these preconditions are usually impossible to fulfill. As long as you define yourself in terms of external achievements or goals, there's really no *you* to love.

You have to be *someone* to become attractive to someone else. You have to be self-accepting before you can please someone you care about. If you don't amount to anything before someone wants you, you won't amount to much afterwards, either.

Three: Attempts to please everyone. Even *thinking* you can satisfy all the people you come across over the course of your life is dangerous.

You must first please yourself. After that, you can work on making the people you care about happy. Beyond that, you're unlikely to do much more than ensure dissatisfaction with yourself, because there's always going to be someone who'll grumble that you're not doing enough. Let them grumble and don't take yourself to task for it. People who try to please everyone end up pleasing no one.

Four: Perfectionism and unrealistic goals. Many people think of themselves as "failures" because they're unable to achieve wildly ambitious objectives. If this describes you, you can improve your performance in any area you choose by starting out with a more modest, attainable goal.

Remember, you can always set a higher goal tomorrow, after you've achieved today's. People don't graduate from college and immediately mount a serious run for president of the United States. There are a few steps that have to be taken in between the two points. Take the same attitude in your relationships. Don't expect your partner to fulfill every dream you've ever had from day one. Start small. Work your way up—together.

Five: Expectations that "the meaning of life" will become clear in a good relationship. Life is not a meaning. It's an opportunity for meaningful experiences. You can only discover *the* ultimate meaning of your life at the end of it.

Don't make the questions too broad or expect the lessons always to be profound. Some of the most profound things about relationships are intimately related to our seemingly mundane, everyday existence. Life is made up of meaningful experiences, not definitive answers. Those experiences are often of short duration, but they can occur again and again . . . and they can make you happy.

Six: Boredom as a way of life. Some people, it seems, find a great deal of pleasure in being bored. How else can you explain their relentless attachment to the very things that bore them?

If you're bored, you're boring to be with. And you're not only boring for *others* to be with—you'll be boring for *you* to be with! If continued attempts to find a passionate, challenging interest lead you nowhere, then, by all means, *fake it* for a while. *Pretend* you're enthralled with what's taking place, and see what happens. Moaning about how you have nothing to do or how uninteresting an activity is will *always* make you less attractive and lower your perceptions of yourself.

Seven: A belief that forces outside of oneself control one's life. It's interesting to note that people who feel this way tend not to take very good care of themselves.

Such attitudes don't do much for the way others look at you, and they certainly don't do much for a healthy self-image. Even though there are uncertainties and experiences over which you have no control in life, ultimately, *you* are responsible for your existence. It has to be you. If it isn't you, if job, family, politics, weather, or anything else has the final word about who you are, what you do, and how you can feel about things, then you've effectively abandoned your life.

The Paradox

Worried about your appearance? Don't start from the outside. Start from the inside.

You can apply all the face cream, deodorant, hair conditioner, and makeup you want—the fact remains you must care about yourself before you can expect mature love in return. This is something of a paradox. Many people are surprised when they learn that the best way to attract someone else is to pay healthy, continuous, non-narcissistic attention to themselves. But it's true.

If you develop a positive self-image, and feel good about yourself, others will find you attractive.

People who feel good about themselves don't exploit others, and aren't available for exploitation. People who feel good about themselves, far from exhausting or trying the patience of their acquaintances, exhibit a veritable feast of exciting, appealing characteristics that other human beings tend to find irresistible.

Here are some of those qualities.

People with high self-esteem . . .

. . . have a sense of humor.

. . . don't exploit others for their own short-term gratification.

. . . have a high energy level.

. . . know how to listen.

. . . are more creative than people with low self-esteem.

. . . are tolerant of the changing moods of others.

. . . learn how to live with what they can't change.

. . . are enthusiastic.

. . . exude self-confidence.

. . . appreciate the successes of their friends without feeling competitive or threatened.

. . . are sympathetic when friends fail.

. . are pleased when they can spend time with loved ones, but don't feel abandoned when this is not possible.

. . are sensitive to the needs of others.

. . . know when to take risks.

. . . often have an intriguing sense of mystery about them.

. . . don't pretend they have all the answers.

. . . are optimistic.

. . . don't insult or make fun of others.

. . . can offer love unselfishly.

. . . tend to make the people they spend time with feel better about themselves.

. . . enjoy helping others.

. . . have a sense of their own special mission in life.

. . . are able to turn their mistakes into lessons and begin anew.

It's all very well to talk about how important it is to develop high self-esteem. . . but actually doing so is difficult for many people. Changes don't happen overnight, but by focusing on attainable goals, you can alter the way you look at yourself.

Perhaps you believe that it would take a miracle for you to fundamentally change the way you look at yourself. Fine. Start by creating that miracle. Recognize that you are unique, that no one else on the face of the earth offers exactly what you do. Send yourself positive messages; believe that you are good enough to stand on your own merits. You'll be fine, and eventually the urge to compare yourself with others will recede. Remember that, whatever their accomplishments or presumed advantages, they can't be you—only you can.

It may be helpful for you to review pertinent sections of this book once again. If you bypassed some suggestions because they didn't seem "worth the trouble," reconsider them. If you attempted one of the activities but lost interest, try again. And while you do your mitzvahs, follow your exercise routine, try to give up smoking, cultivate a hobby, or whatever, keep in mind the old Zen expression: "When the mind is ready, a teacher appears."

You can be your own teacher. Are you ready?

Chapter Seven:
Sex—How Important Is It?

IN CONTEMPORARY AMERICAN society, sex has been ruthlessly commercialized, consistently overstated in relation to its actual role in our lives, and shamelessly sensationalized at every opportunity.

Is it any wonder many of us are confused about our sexuality?

We are bombarded daily with titillating sexual messages and stereotypes. The sources are legion: billboard after billboard, commercial after commercial, rock video after rock video, book after book, and film after film, we are constantly being told, directly or indirectly, that sex constitutes the most significant aspect of modern life.

The irony is that the vast majority of the messages we receive are to a large degree *anti-sexual* in nature. Why? Because most of the images the media presents us with have nothing to do with ordinary, healthy sexual experiences.

Think about it. It's extremely rare for, say, a television drama to treat the topics of love and sexual expression in a mature, enlightened way. Much more common are the portrayals of people as lustful or childish buffoons in their relationships, with the accent, wherever possible, on the exploitative aspects of sexuality. Rape, adultery, sadomasochism, and violence get far more attention than caring, compassionate interactions.

Particularly troubling is the advertising industry's seemingly unquenchable desire to establish and reinforce impossible standards of physical allure and sexual persuasiveness. To take the advertisers at face value is to believe that every woman must be stunningly (and identically) beautiful, that every man will seduce an attractive woman given the slightest chance, and that only the purchase of the toothpaste, perfume, clothing, or cosmetic in question will allow one to lead a satisfying sex life.

Perhaps it's because of such messages that so many people use sex as a bargaining tool, or (just as troubling) as a way to avoid intimacy, rather than express it. Many people in our society simply reject sex as a pleasurable, sharing experience, opting instead to use it to prove "manhood" or "femininity," or to try to satisfy deep-seated desires related to being wanted or valid as a person.

That such approaches to sexuality are still common is disturbing, and, considering the recent upswings in the rate and severity of sexually transmitted diseases, downright alarming.

Don't misunderstand me. In the broad sense, all of us are sexual in many, many aspects of life, and sexuality *is* of great importance to us as men and women—but it needs to be viewed in perspective, as one of the many dimensions of our existence. As I've already indicated, I believe that of the ten most important aspects of a relationship, sex ranks ninth. (Most couples in a happy, mature relationship will tell you that the *real* turn-on is intimacy, and that love and caring can, in their own ways, be more rewarding and exciting than the simple act of intercourse.)

There are, in my opinion, four key ideas that will help us to put sex into its proper perspective; in this chapter, we'll look at each in detail.

Four Guidelines

One: Sexual intercourse is neither a test nor a proof of love. I've mentioned this before, but the point is so routinely ignored that it bears repeating. Caring about each other, sharing unselfishly, developing respect for your partner—these are the things that will help you build a strong relationship, one that will stand the test of time. Simply going to bed together will, on its own, prove nothing.

It's quite common today for couples to undergo serious crises that have at their root a confusion of the ideas of sex and love.

Perhaps the most familiar example of this is the teenaged couple entering the first stages of sexual experimentation. The young woman is told by her partner that if she "really" loved him, she'd have sex. If the young man's demands don't confuse sex with love, nothing does.

There are other such scenarios. Consider the case of a young, happily married couple who've just celebrated their first anniversary, and, after a full year of trying, are still unable to achieve simultaneous orgasms (an unrealistic goal for most couples). They consider this a slowly-worsening catastrophe. Do they really love each other after all? Did they make some terrible mistake in getting married?

Or how about the couple, happily married for fifteen years, who have the misfortune to read about the newest trendy "disease" to make an appearance in the newsweeklies—lack of interest in sex? How often, they now ask themselves, *do* we make love, anyway . . .? Good God! Here they thought they were a contented couple! They were foolish enough to believe that the steady growth of intimacy, understanding, and caring they'd experienced was a good sign. Now they're asked to believe that those things only masked some terrible disorder that is now keeping them from having the right amount of sex together! (Of course, there is no "right" amount of lovemaking, and the couple described has no need to consult a sex therapist or marriage counselor.)

Sex and love, then, must not be confused. It's a good idea to remember that there are people who have perfectly good, or even ecstatic, sexual relationships with partners they loathe. There are also couples who are very deeply in love, but whose sex lives aren't particularly satisfying for them because of problems such as impotence, inability to reach orgasm, or premature ejaculation. And yes, there are even people (wonder of wonders!) who have completely mature, exciting relationships with no such physical problems, in which sexual intercourse occurs rarely and is of minimal consequence.

Of course, millions of well-adjusted couples enjoy buoyant, frequent sexual intercourse as part of a well-rounded, caring, and intimate relationship. But that does not mean that the fact that they love their partners is any guarantee of ongoing sexual frequency or satisfaction.

Two: There's absolutely nothing wrong with waiting until you're married to have sex. Nevertheless, some important facts should be taken into account. Firstly, if you do decide to wait, you're very definitely in the minority. It's been estimated that less than one-tenth of all newlyweds are both virgins on their wedding night. The National Center for Health Statistics reported in 1985 that four out of five women had sex before marriage. And my own work suggests that something in the neighborhood of ninety percent of all men are sexually active before they're married.

In addition, if you decide to postpone sex until marriage, you must be prepared for the possibility that the earth will not move nor the skies part on that first night. If you expect to have simultaneous orgasms the first time, you're likely to come away from the experience feeling an emotion something akin to, "For *this* I waited?"

Sexual technique is something people learn, not something they're born with, and first experiences tend to be grim for both sexes. The standard reactions for most men after first coitus is that the experience was embarrassing; for most women, that it was painful.

Finally, let me caution you against the double standard in this area. It is foolish and unfair to reduce a potential partner to a category by placing undue emphasis on whether or not he or she is a virgin.

After one of my lectures, a young man approached me and, after some discussion about what makes for a satisfying relationship, the conversation turned to his marital plans. I asked him what kind of person would make him happy, and he immediately ruled out any woman with any prior sex whatsoever. "I'm a man," he said, "so naturally I fool around, but when I get married I'm going to settle down with a virgin."

"I hope," I told him, "that you'll marry a person, and not a hymen."

Three: Partners can only learn the most important things about sex from each other, and that means good communication is essential. Not too long ago, a woman who'd been married for ten years complained to me that she'd never had an orgasm because her husband had no idea how to stimulate her. "Why don't you show him how?" I asked. "Oh, I couldn't," she replied; "I don't want to hurt his feelings."

I'm all for tact and politeness, but basic human needs are basic human needs, and if they're consistently ignored, something's very wrong somewhere. Specifically, something's probably wrong with this couple's communication skills.

Are you hesitant about discussing what does or does not satisfy you sexually? Do you (or would you) rebuff your partner's attempts to communicate about the subject? Do you think that sex "takes care of itself" without either partner having to provide feedback? If so, you may be on the road to a crisis—one you can easily avoid.

Once you can talk openly about your reactions to sex, you and your partner will have opened up a new world of intimacy and

togetherness. Doing so is worth the initial feelings of awkward-
ness and risk, which usually pass in time.

*Four: The best way to test any relationship's potential is to postpone
having sex.* It's true. What do you do in the meantime? Plenty!

Sexual intercourse, as you've probably gathered by now, is not
the only way people express their sexuality. The other options
are virtually limitless. Hugging, kissing, foot or body massages,
long walks holding hands (yes, I said "holding hands"), all are
among the many other healthy ways to express physical attraction. Take advantage of them.

Ann Landers, in a recent column, wrote about the thousands
upon thousands of letters she'd received from women who
claimed they'd gladly give up sex if they could be sure of receiv-
ing from their partners, in exchange, satisfying levels of "non-
sex" physical affection: caresses, kisses, hugs. Of course, most
women would prefer both sex and intimacy. But apparently the
letter-writers were getting quite enough sex and not enough of
what they really wanted—the caring and tenderness so often
absent from coitus alone.

It's also interesting to note that the treatment of choice for
people who have sexual problems is not to have sex for a month
or longer. During that time, the couple builds communication
skills, talks about what is or is not satisfying physically about
their lovemaking, and tries out alternative expressions of sexuality like the ones outlined above. Most important, the partners have the chance to discover (or rediscover) the beauty and
wonder of each other's personalities.

Sex: The Lifelong Learning Experience

I'd like to offer a few more important points on the larger issue
of human sexuality itself. I should point out, though, that the
topic as a whole is vast and, from the individual's standpoint,
ever-changing. Sex is a lifelong learning experience, one which
can't be completely and fully addressed in any book, much less

these few pages. (For more in-depth approaches, consult the Bibliography.) What follows, then, are brief (and, I hope, helpful) observations on some of the more important questions and problems relating to individual sexuality today.

Fantasies

For starters, let's talk about fantasies. Many people are curious about their sexual fantasies, but never work up the necessary courage or feel comfortable enough to ask the question that's on their minds: Is what I'm thinking normal?

The answer, thankfully, is yes. Behavior, of course, can be wrong, but thoughts by themselves cannot. We all have weird thoughts, dreams, fantasies, wishes, or sexual desires. They often come from the unconscious levels of the mind, leaving us with little or no control over the way they emerge in our consciousness. That's okay.

If you feel guilty about a particular turn-on, it will probably repeat itself for as long as you continue to tell yourself that the thought was "wrong." Why? Guilt is the driving force, the energy in the repetition of unacceptable thoughts.

Once you realize that all your fantasies, no matter how off-the-wall, are a normal part of human existence, they'll pass harmlessly and give you no further trouble.

In *my* fantasy life, I'm a "tri-sexual"; I've tried everything. But like most people, I draw a clear line between the real world (in which my actions must be responsible ones) and the world of dreams and desires.

Of course, when normal thoughts are translated into obsessions, they can influence you negatively, or upset the regular pattern of your life. Nevertheless, it's the *behavior* accompanying obsession that needs to be controlled, not the fantasy.

Teen Sex

In my view, it's perfectly all right to discourage teenagers from having sex.

Why am I against teen sex? As a rule, teenagers are too young, too vulnerable, and far too likely to end up the victims of abuse or exploitation. Furthermore, when they have sex, they tend not to use contraceptives.

Teenagers represent the group most likely to be unable to handle the consequences of a sexual relationship. If you feel the same way, and want to make early efforts to avoid future crises, you may want to read my book, *Raising A Child Conservatively In A Permissive World* (Fireside, 1986).

Penis Size: It Means Less Than You Think

Freud may have gotten it wrong when he wrote about women having penis envy. In contemporary society, it seems, only men have it.

Penis size is, in virtually all cases, unrelated to sexual gratification, no matter what you hear, and no matter how sensitive some men are about the issue. (To be fair, sometimes women reinforce feelings of insecurity about genital size by making thoughtless or cruel comments.)

Size is not what counts. The desire to satisfy each other is what counts. Furthermore, one cannot tell the size of the penis by observing its non-erect state. Some appear small and erect to six inches; some appear large and erect to five and a half inches. One size, as it were, fits all.

Along the same lines, it's worth noting that a mature vagina can't be "too small." After all, a *baby* comes out of the vagina! While tension or nervousness may be the cause of enough tightness or rigidity to make sex difficult, no vagina is "too small" for a penis.

Sexual Gamesmanship

While more and more people these days are making a commitment to genuine compassion and caring in their relationships, there's still quite a lot of game-playing when it comes to sex. How do you respond to these games?

In my book *Seduction Lines Heard 'Round the World (And Answers You Can Give)* (Prometheus, 1987), I collected hundreds of the lines used by men and women to seduce one another (though men still lead the field in this area). I also supplied some comebacks for use in responding to these lines.

Here are some examples.

C'mon; everybody is doing it.
Good. Then you won't have any trouble finding someone else to do it with.

Where have you been all my life?
Hiding from you.

I can't use a condom. I get no feeling that way.
That's strange; all the other guys I know get plenty of feeling wearing a condom.

If I put on a condom, I won't get the right sensation out of our lovemaking.
If you don't put on a condom, you won't get any sensation at all.

Don't worry about birth control. I'll just stay in for a minute.
What do you think I am, a microwave oven?

Sexual Problems and Your Relationship

Many people make themselves unavailable as long-term or marital partners because of sexually related problems. Often, this reaction is overhasty and leads to unnecessary discontentment.

For men, the problems usually center around anxiety over sexual performance, resulting in impotence or premature ejaculation. For women, it's mainly fear (or outright terror) of making love traceable to a traumatic sexual history, perhaps including rape, molestation, or simply repeated deception, cruelty, or rejection in past relationships. (Inability to achieve orgasm, in and of itself, is not usually reason enough to dissuade a woman from a relationship or marriage.)

If you have a sex problem, the best approach is to acknowledge your insecurities and anxieties early on in a relationship. If you and your partner like each other, enjoy each other's company, and consider each other potential mates, it's appropriate to be honest about your situation. Say something like, "I want to be up front with you from the very beginning; I have a problem with sex. My anxiety (or: past experience) keeps me from performing the way I want to. Eventually, I'd like to get close—physically intimate—with you. But I don't want to try having sexual intercourse until I reach a comfort level that permits it."

You'd be surprised how many men and women will find this acceptable. Many couples adapt to this arrangement much more easily than they might to, say, a single experience of impotence, or pain upon attempting intercourse. As we know, the lack of sexual intercourse does not mean that you cannot express your sexuality in other ways. You should also remember that a relationship without sex (even for an extended period) is not necessarily a bitter or unpleasant one; only when one partner feels ignored, ungratified, or unfulfilled does the lack of sexual desire or performance become an issue.

If your partner has a sex problem, try to remember that the vast majority of the disturbances are primarily of psychological origin. (There are, however, some medical exceptions: certain types of impotence, for instance.) As such, the problems are usually subject to cure and even complete recovery. It's your job to assure your partner of this—and to be patient. Be flexible. If you love your partner, it will be worth it to try to work the problems out.

Concentrate on developing a sensuous and erotic relationship, not on coitus itself. Try innovative approaches: massage, mutual masturbation, or other ideas from the many books and manuals available today. If and only if this approach does not work after a few months, you might want to consider sex therapy.

The Penis: Does It Have a Life of Its Own?

Women are often surprised to learn that many males feel that their penises are not subject to their wishes, that the male genitals are often seen as being "out of control."

In counseling situations, some men reveal that they undergo "power struggles" between the penis and willpower, frequently attributing to their genitals undesirable attributes unrelated to their conscious intent. "The penis," they've been known to say, "seems to have a mind of its own."

Of course, each of us is responsible for our own acts. Men who separate their conscious will from the seemingly independent and often exploitative impulses associated with their genitals are usually engaging in rationalization and denial. When a behavior becomes addictive or involuntary—such as habitual rape or child molestation, or constant preoccupation with pornography—the penis itself may be a convenient scapegoat, and may be assigned the role of the perpetrator, unaccountable and out of control.

In the absence of such rationalizations, however, the idea is not so far-fetched. It's true that erections sometimes occur without apparent conscious stimulation, i.e., when a father wrestles with his children, or when a heterosexual man showers with a muscular male friend. Virtually every male has experienced arousal without having planned for or encouraged it at some point in his life.

It's not entirely clear just why men have erections associated with events or fantasies that are foreign (or even antithetical) to conscious motives and values, but they do. Men involved in workplace "power play" confrontations with female colleagues have been known to become aroused without any conscious awareness of a sexual interest in the coworker. Still more curious is the common (but rarely discussed) phenomenon of a man being "unwittingly" aroused by incest, rape, or dismemberment fantasies that run counter to every basic value he holds.

Strange as such arousals may sound not only to women, but to the men who experience them, in the majority of cases they represent no cause for alarm. If these "dark urges" do not result in inappropriate behavior, and are not symptomatic of other neurotic problems, they may simply reflect a normal range of sexual functioning and need not be viewed with concern.

A more serious dilemma is the socialization many men receive that, once an erection starts and sexual tension is maintained, there is simply no turning back. Much of what is now identified as "date rape" is rooted in the erroneous assumption that once a man is sexually aroused in the presence of his desired sex object, he can't stop, and must act on the arousal. The man may, afterwards, blame the woman for "encouraging him," often along the lines of, "Well, why did you invite me in? You said hello, didn't you? Why did you kiss me? Why did you give me a drink?" In these instances, as well, rationalization and denial are at the forefront.

Men can stop. The notion that they can't is reinforced in some men by the development of "blue balls" (a pain in the genitals associated with unreleased sexual tension), but masturbation provides instant relief. There is absolutely no physical damage or harm sustained when an aroused man does not "score." The main barrier men in this situation face is the dangerous and nonsensical idea that rape or even sexual molestation is preferable to masturbation.

The organ that really controls the penis is the brain, not the other way around (though it should be recognized that not all aspects of the brain are subject to conscious control). To be sure, there's nothing wrong with a man scolding, waxing philosophical with, or awarding more credit than deserved to his penis. And, as we'll see in the following paragraphs, there's also nothing wrong with masturbating joyfully when the penis seems to be getting the better of an argument.

Masturbation

Masturbation is a healthy, normal outlet for adolescents, adult singles, and even married people (particularly when opportunities for sex with the spouse are temporarily unavailable). Especially when it comes to married couples, however, there remains some resistence to the idea that masturbation can be a part of a well-adjusted sex life. But think about it: What are the partners supposed to do when one must, say, go away on a business trip for three weeks? Have affairs? For my money, masturbation represents a far healthier and realistic option in a mature relationship. (It's worth noting, too, that masturbation is the treatment of choice for women who have trouble reaching an orgasm.)

Almost all males masturbate at some time during their lives. About three-quarters of women do the same. Nowadays, modern mothers tell their children that it's okay to play with themselves, as long as they do it in private, and not too much. This certainly represents a healthier approach to the matter than was in fashion some years ago (when it was widely believed that "self-abuse" brought in its wake acne, tired blood, heartburn, and, in extreme cases, blindness). But think about it from the child's point of view for a moment: How much is too much? Once a year? Twice a year? After every meal?

The simplest and most honest approach with children is to tell them the truth. Once is too much if you don't like it. If you don't like it, don't do it; otherwise don't worry about it.

As with any activity, masturbation can become neurotic or compulsive. There are people who eat too much because of high anxiety levels, and people who drink too much for the same reason. It would be remarkable indeed if the same weren't true of masturbating.

Granted. Some people do indeed masturbate compulsively, as a response to anxiety. My feeling, though, is that if you absolutely must have a compulsion, masturbation is probably one of the best ones going. While many people die every year of excessive drug, alcohol, or food intake, the record has yet to show a case of someone dying from over-masturbation. Masturbation, frankly, is the compulsion of choice, with the highest potential for enjoyment and least harm to oneself or to others. You could call it the cost-effective compulsion.

If your religion frowns on masturbation, it probably won't do you any harm to avoid it. But please be careful what you tell yourself or your children about self-stimulation. Where people run into genuine problems is not with masturbation itself, but with the guilt that becomes associated with it, particularly when a child is punished for the activity. It's possible for some people to live a completely celibate life and be completely happy; I doubt seriously, though, that it can be accomplished if a person feels guilt or shame about one's sexuality. In all the work I've done and all the research I've compiled with reference to rape and sexual molestation of children, I've never come across a male perpetrator who was comfortable about masturbation while growing up.

And, while we're on that serious subject . . .

The Abuser—and the Abused

If you were sexually molested as a child, you must do whatever is necessary to come to terms with the experience and convince yourself that it was not your fault. The reason for this is very simple.

It wasn't.

Whether you resisted or not, whether you told someone or not, whether you liked it or not, sexual molestation of children is the responsibility of the adults who initate it. Always. The adult knows the activity is wrong. The child is a victim.

Unfortunately for the victim, much work usually remains to be done after the fact. If you fall into this category, you must recover from any guilt feelings and learn not to punish yourself. If you don't recover, you run the risk of becoming a perpetual victim; in a sense, you "marry" your victimizer. Don't do it. Separate yourself from the victimizer. Living well is the best revenge. (Those men who've been molested as children should be especially vigilant about getting help *at all costs,* especially if there's an urge to repeat the cycle and molest others. If you have this tendency, please get help before you find yourself in serious trouble.)

The same advice applies for those adults who have been raped. The proper mental attitude will go a long way toward helping you to deal with the trauma in a healthy way. The rape was not your fault, in just the same way that it would not be your fault if you were mugged. If you need support on the road to recovery (and it's a good bet that you will), you might decide, eventually, to help others who've had a similar experience. Join a support group or help in a rape crisis center. Why punish yourself twice by maintaining an emotional involvement with the person who hurt you?

Homosexuality

About six percent of men are predominantly gay; about four percent of women are predominantly lesbian. No one knows the "cause," any more than the "cause" of heterosexuality is known.

All that's certain is that a person's sexual orientation is pretty much determined by the time he or she is three to four years old, and that sexual orientation is not a matter of rational choice.

Many people discover they are homosexual in the late adolescent and early adult years, sometimes after marriage. Some homosexuals marry in an attempt to "cure" themselves, but this rarely works.

A few homosexual experiences or fantasies, or the fact that you are approached by a homosexual, does not mean that you are a homosexual. (According to Kinsey, some 37 percent of all males have had at least one homosexual experience to a point of ejaculation.) What *is* a homosexual? From a pragmatic point of view, the best definition is a person who, as an adult, feels him or herself irresistibly attracted to, and has sex with, someone of the same sex.

These are not easy times to be lesbian or gay. Many extremists have taken public concern over the spread of the AIDS virus as a cue to vent their spleen against homosexuals without fear of encountering mainstream opposition. That many of these extremists spread panic, prejudice, and fear in a religious context is one of the most troubling elements of contemporary life. Bigots, however, will be bigots, even if they stand behind a pulpit.

Most of the logic the extremists offer in defense of their anti-homosexual attitudes simply does not stand scrutiny. When someone argues seriously to me that God has visited His retribution on gays, and that He gave them AIDS as punishment for their immorality, my response is to ask whether God has it in for Legionnaires as well. After all, He gave them Legionnaire's disease! And if God is so angry at homosexuals, why has He not ensured that lesbians, along with gay men and intravenous drug users, are counted among the major risk groups?

"Safer Sex"

Unless you are absolutely sure that both partners are virgins, and utterly confident that neither partner will sleep with someone else while your relationship is going on, I strongly recommend that you use the "safer sex" methods designed to address the increasingly serious problem of sexually transmitted diseases, including AIDS. (In addition, of course, an intelligent selection of birth control methods will reduce the likelihood of unwanted pregnancy.)

Some experts suggest that using the diaphragm in conjuntion with both spermicide and a condom is the safest method. Though the only completely safe approach to sex is abstinence, there is, today, no excuse for engaging in sexual intercourse while having taken insufficient precautions where health and birth control are concerned.

Here are some other guidelines I recommend you follow if your sex partner is not your long-term monogamous lover.

Avoid anal sex. With or without a condom. (Receptive anal sex represents, for homosexuals, the activity with the greatest risk for transmission of the human immunodeficiency, or HIV, virus.)

Avoid oral sex. Or at least stop before ejaculation.

Be sure that neither you nor your partner has sex with prostitutes, intravenous drug users, or male homosexuals who have had sexual relations in the last seven years. Sexual intercourse with risk group members increases your chances of picking up the virus.

Do not engage in one night stands. Remember that when you sleep with someone "casually," you are usually unaware of whether or not his or her partners were in AIDS risk groups; you may be exposing yourself to the virus.

As serious as the AIDS epidemic is, it does not, alas, represent the only threat to your health related to sex.

All sexually transmitted diseases require medical treatment, but a special caution is probably in order when discussing herpes. It is estimated that more than thirty million Americans have genital herpes, which, as of late 1988, is still an incurable disease. While herpes is most commonly transmitted from a partner who has active lesions, it can also be infectious when there are no obvious symptoms. Therefore, condoms and spermicides should also be used when a partner has herpes, even if there are no visual clues that the lesions are in an active state.

If you have genital herpes, you are strongly urged not to have sex until you've established a mature relationship and informed your partner about the precautions which must be taken. Once the proper steps are followed, there is relatively little risk to the sexual health of someone who sleeps with a person who has herpes. Even before you make love, it's best to be honest early on in the relationship about your condition to avoid later problems.

For more information on how to manage these situations, write the Herpes Resource Center, P.O. Box 13827, Research Triangle Park, NC 27709. (Enclose a self-addressed business envelope with two first-class stamps.)

Chapter Eight: Preparing for the Responsibility of Family Life — An Emerging View for Marriages in the 1990's

WHILE MANY MYTHS and illusions still surround the marital relationship, expectations associated with marriage seem somehow to have become more realistic in recent years. Most couples now realize that when they marry, they aren't wedding a perfect individual. Reasons for marriage beyond financial security or sexual gratification are more common than they were a generation or so ago. People are more likely to accept that love will not remain forever unchanged in its intensity, and to recognize the need for two people to work together through the inevitable difficult periods.

Certainly, no one will deny that these are healthy developments. The fact is, love often undergoes periods of indifference and animosity; some marriages even seem to have the effect of moving the partners further apart rather than bringing them closer. In any event, a long-term relationship, and specifically a marriage, is usually fluid and changing. If there's a couple whose true feelings never change from a constant, gleeful state of affection, I haven't come across them yet.

Do you remember how intense it felt to be in love at, say, age sixteen? Like most people, you were probably so overwhelmed by the experience that you couldn't think of anyone other than your beloved and couldn't bear to be separated for the shortest periods of time. You may even have had difficulty sleeping.

Those kinds of strong feelings during adolescence tend to last for only a short time. The "undying love" dies and is, in short order, replaced by a new "undying love." That process, perhaps embarrassing to you now in retrospect, is in fact an essential part of growing up.

Unfortunately, there are still many people who marry with the notion that the honeymoon will last forever. Trying to make the first rush of "undying love" a permanent marital environment is not only unrealistic, but is also bound to be a source of disappointment and frustration.

Moments of Joy

The most meaningful experiences in life all tend to be of brief duration. Consider the things you enjoy most—orgasms, sunsets, plays, a child's first words. How long do they last? Just imagine how bored and exhausted you'd be if you actually made the superhuman effort necessary to attempt to prolong any of those activities into a full day, sunup to sundown. And imagine how unnatural and empty the experience would be if you could somehow succeed in doing so.

Marriages are the same way. There are moments of dissatisfaction. And there are moments of joy.

Many couples married for some time complain that their intimacies and feelings for each other have become monotonous. Perhaps they have fallen into the routine of making love at certain times and at a certain frequency. For some, the act loses its imaginative qualities and becomes a mere repetition of worn-out positions and techniques.

Other couples, married just as long, are able to bring moments of spontaneity and joy to lovemaking that allow them to relive the joy of their commitment. They may not make love five times a week. But they retain those exciting moments.

Myths

Some people would have you believe that marital love and companionship within the strict limits of the pair-bond should satisfy an individual's every emotional, physical, social, and intellectual need. Couples who try to live this myth share all the same friends and discard those who don't get along with both partners, abandon long-held interests or hobbies because the spouse does not share them, and generally maintain a "couple front" wherever they go. They signal to all outsiders that each partner is off limits to any activity unless both show enthusiasm for it.

While sharing *no* interests and spending little time together is an equally harmful extreme, the "couple trap" I've just outlined is not recommended for any relationship. Complete possessiveness in the name of love has two troubling effects. First, it stifles individual expression and creativity. At the same time, it places unrealistic limitations on a couple's range of experience. Shared *values* are crucial; identical *interests* are not.

Almost all of us are dependent on other people for our emotional and physical well-being. Within the framework of the more overburdened and overdependent relationships, however, dependency can resuilt in unrealistic expectations and, often, a seemingly endless wellspring of hurt feelings. Partners realize before long that one person simply cannot "mean everything."

Toward Egalitarian Marriages

Some men say they like a "traditional" marriage setting—one with rigidly defined gender roles—because each partner "knows what has to be done." And there is a regularity to these marriages; the husband works, the wife handles most of the domestic duties.

But intimacy and caring frequently evaporate when a marriage is reduced to a series of chores and nothing more. Many of these men reserve Monday as their football night, Tuesday as their bowling night, Wednesday as their night "out with the boys". . . .

They're just not around a lot. The truth is, they find their marriages boring, and they're unwilling to work to change things. They avoid contact in any number of ways. They may still have sex with their wives, but they're rarely intimate. Many women feel that their roles in such marriages are unchallenging and repetitive, that there are few options for self-expression in *their* lives. (On the other hand, "traditional" marriages do work well for many men and women, despite the unflattering generalizations I've put forth.)

Slowly, society has moved more and more toward egalitarian marriages, toward settings that encourage differences in taste and opinion without threatening the core of the relationship—intimacy and commitment. The simple fact is, people who are self-fulfilled and who maintain and develop their own friends are happier than people who don't.

Both partners in a marriage should be able to minimize the repetitive, routine elements of life, and enjoy the presence of a sense of possibility and imagination. Such a shared commitment provides variation, and keeps partners from becoming cynical about the relationship.

Today's marriage partners must accept that life is not automatically exciting, that having fun is a privilege accorded to those who are willing to think creatively about their surroundings. A mutual commitment to make the "daily routine" more of a surprise for both partners will go a long way toward providing marital stability and happiness.

Conflict

Occasional antagonistic episodes between spouses are a fact of life. Yet people often become extremely defensive and anxious when told that their mate can be expected to go through periods of indifference (or even hate) in the relationship.

If the expectations are that no conflicts will ever arise, there's going to be some disappointment. Over time, "buried" resentments and frustrations may resurface in hardened, uncompromising forms that cast a deep tinge of hostility on the relationship. This can be a difficult trend to reverse. In such an environment, many married couples tend to view their initial vows to love one another "till death do us part" as a burdensome responsibility.

It's best to accept the fact that your marriage will have good days and bad days, that occasional fights are *healthy* components of any relationship, and that, in the long run, if your relationship is a mature one, your partner will be around next week even if he or she was out of sorts this morning.

Goodbye to the Stereotypes, But . . .

The strict gender-based societal roles that used to dictate the terms of most marriages are rapidly becoming things of the past. This is a healthy development that promises to help bring greater variety, challenge, and long-term happiness to most marriages.

While the stereotypes may be on their way out, many of the attitudes that supported them remain. Optimally, marital responsibility is based on a mutual desire to meet the other partner's needs. If you learn to view your spouse's needs as demands, you aren't likely to enjoy fulfilling them.

If you demand that I cook your favorite meal and threaten to withhold a similar pleasure unless I comply, I'll begrudge you the favor. But if I'm asked in a pleasant manner—if you speak to me as though you were addressing an equal, and not an errant child—we'll both enjoy ourselves. I'll make you the meal, not because I have to, but because I enjoy doing so and because I love you. Pleasing each other thus becomes an opportunity for mutual giving, not and act of submission or conquest.

Along the same lines, helping out around the house is no fun when it descends into the deadening realm of mindless routine. If it is always my turn to clean the cat box, and if this is a task I find distasteful, after a while the soiled cat box will become a source of genuine resentment. Agreeing to alternate tasks—even if you've had a hard day when your turn comes around—will help remove the monotony of domestic duties.

Such changes, though they tend to focus on "little things," can bring new zest and interest to a marriage. They'll also reduce potential areas of tension in marriages that are closer to the "traditional" way of doing things than they are to the two-career mode. Many women feel a new sense of worth when they demonstrate to themselves and their husbands that they keep house by choice, not because they're incapable of doing other things.

Try to promote a sense of equality. When men and women can come together as equals—not as provider/consumer or leader/follower—they improve their relationships. The best environment for growth is one in which each partner feels as competent and in control of life as the other.

Marriage: Out of Style?

Many contemporary commentators question the future of the institution of marriage. Some claim that the duration of even meaningful relationships is becoming, on average, shorter. The reasons cited include peoples' increased tendency to move frequently, the fact that many of us hold our jobs for shorter periods of time than our parents did, and the rapidly changing values and interests of people in our society.

Perhaps intimacy and really getting to know other people *are* more difficult these days. Certainly, there has been a proliferation of short-term relationships, many with the professed goal of getting the "barrier" of sex out of the way early on. And it is perhaps a little too fashionable these days to make excuses or convincing rationalizations for infidelity or adultery.

But generalizing in this area isn't a profitable exercise. No rigid notions about what relationships are or aren't going through can fully account for the fact that each couple is unique. There are people in monogamous relationships of thirty or forty years' duration who are positively hateful to each other; there are a fair number of not entirely "faithful" couples who love each other a great deal.

The important fact to bear in mind is that no matter how fast-paced or challenging the demands of today's world become, there is nothing inherently boring about monogamy. If you put in the time and caring required to allow mutual trust to grow in your marriage, the relationship will make you happy and keep you interested. And once you and your partner have developed good communication skills, together you can probably satisfy most of the needs you identify.

Stepparenting

If you marry a divorced or widowed person, stepparenting could be in your future. Stepparents often must play a challenging role in today's families, particularly when the biological parent is still alive (as is usually the case). If you are about to enter this situation, there are a number of problems you may encounter.

Though there are undoubtedly many, many families that integrate a stepparenting situation successfully, as a general rule, stepparents face tougher challenges than other family members.

Stepparenting is *not* just like being a "normal" parent, nor is it equivalent to adopting a child. A stepmother or stepfather who tries to adjust to an existing family unit faces a far different situation than just about any other type of relative; specifically, the stepparent must confront the fact that others may perceive him or her as a "replacement," and deal with the (understandable) resentment that often accompanies this perception.

Here are some tips that will help you approach the experience of stepparenting, and can assist you in making the transition into a fulfilling, satisfying family life.

It's usually a good idea to expect that the children will harbor some resentment, and will consciously or unconsciously try to put you on the defensive and test your limits. It's not reasonable to expect a child to understand fully the situation that led to the divorce or death of the "real parent." Unfavorable comparisons are to be expected.

In addition, your stepchildren may have feelings of resentment or anger stemming from the perception that you, a relative newcomer, now appear to have priority when it comes to your partner's time, affection, or money. Some stepchildren even cross the line between passive dissatisfaction and make active attempts to cause the marriage to fail. Such efforts may be sparked by presumed unequal treatment by the parent, or perhaps over something as seemingly trivial as a new living arrangement (which might, for instance, force two children to share what had been one person's room). Then, of course, there are the difficult instances in which a child tries to make a marriage fail in the hope of seeing the original set of parents reunited.

One point frequently overlooked in all this is the fact that children as a whole, and stepchildren in particular, are, like all of us, influenced by genetic as well as environmental factors. These factors can influence a child in ways that the stepparent may not always be able to control or understand. Some children will never feel love for the new parent (just as as some stepparents will not able to feel love for some children). In these cases, "trying hard enough" becomes an academic concern; love cannot be mandated. Failing to accept such circumstances can lead to unnecessary feelings of guilt or rage; in many families, inappropriate behavior such as overaggressiveness, contempt, or pity may follow.

In general, it's best to operate on the assumption that the child doesn't have to love you or even get along well with you. It's good to keep this in mind at all times, but it's especially important when dealing with direct challenges along the lines of, "You're not my mother (father)—I don't have to love you!" (Of course, no one's saying that dealing with such situations will be easy. be easy. Your best response to such an outburst may be something like this: "I know you don't have to, and it's okay if you don't want to love me. Perhaps I don't even deserve your love, but I think it would be easier for us if we could get along better.")

When, as a stepparent, you must play the role of the disciplinarian, you will have to walk a particularly fine line. Do not require that the stepchild obey you out of respect for your authority or love for you as a family member; you can't count on either one existing, particularly in the early stages. *Never* give in to the temptation to use threats like, "If you don't take out the garbage, I'm telling your father!"

Questions Stepparents Ask . . .
And Some Possible Answers

Sometimes I feel such hostility from my stepchildren. One minute they're hugging me and the next minute they're giving me the cold shoulder. How should I handle this?

Accept it. This is the real world, and sometimes people's emotions change. If you feel it's a serious problem, you might want to bring it up at a time when the child is feeling affectionate towards you.

My four-year-old stepson recently looked up at me and said, "My mom-my says you're not my real stepmother until she dies." I didn't know what to say. Do you?

How about, "That's all right, dear. She is your real mother; but we both care about you."

How can I minimize the initial tension that builds up in the first hour or so when my stepchildren visit for the weekend?

Arrange for activities (such as movies, games, or visits with friends) that don't require you to "make conversation." Let the relationship and the discussions develop slowly.

Why do I sometimes feel I have to do better than my stepchildren's real mother?

Why you feel that way is not as important as how you deal with the feeling. Tell yourself, "I'll do the best I can." Sometimes even the best we can do doesn't produce the results we might want.

I married a woman with three kids . . . my first marriage. Lately, my wife has been subtly putting pressure on me to play my part in the "one big happy family" cast. I think she's trying to compensate for what was missing from her last marriage. I understand what she's trying to do, but it's making me resent the kids and I've even begun pushing her away, too. What should I do?

Suggest to your wife that her efforts are not realistic, but make every effort to maintain a good, genuine relationship with the kids. Why punish them? If the situation seems to be deteriorating, counseling would probably be the best approach.

I'm planning to marry a woman with two children. They want to call me "Dad," but I don't feel that I'm ready for that. Any suggestions?

Let them call you "Dad." Seriously, what's the big deal? The problem is usually the other way around—children are often understandably hesitant in reassigning their affections. As an adult in the family, you should be willing to make some compromises. If you really feel it's a problem, talk to them. But such issues are more important, in the long run, to the children than to you. Try to let them decide. Give the situation time.

Everyone Learns

There's no denying that stepparenting can be difficult. By the same token, the family that incorporates a stepparent enjoys unique opportunities for growth on the part of both the parents and the children. Children may have additional adult role models to whom they can look for guidance and motivation. The act of creatively resolving the inevitable conflicts can be a learning experience for everyone in the family. Furthermore, "dual-family" situations, in which there are more than the customary two parents, allows for a domestic environment in which no parent has a monopoly on the provision of all emotional or financial "raw materials."

Even bearing all this in mind, you may still approach the prospect of entering "someone else's family" with some trepidation. Luckily, if you plan to become a stepparent, you are not alone. One or more children living with a stepparent and a natural parent is a characteristic household in about 10 percent of all American families; it's estimated that there are some twelve million stepparents in the United States. It's likely that you have a friend or relative in a parallel situation to whom you can turn for more advice.

How Not to Define Love . . .
And How to Teach Your Children
Once You've Finished Not Defining It

Many people try to "nail down" exactly what love "means" so they can use the definition to help them find the solutions to problems in their marriages or relationships. The efforts are usually fruitless.

The popular formula "Love is . . ." is nothing more than a catch phrase popular with writers and speakers eager to capitalize on the public's hunger for easy answers to difficult questions. The very fact that hundreds of phrases have been used to complete the sentence should give some indication of the difficulty of coming across a truly authoritative definition.

Love is not an ending point. It's a starting point. To love truly, you have to start by loving yourself. Believe that you are a worthwhile human being with valid feelings, thoughts, and behaviors that you accept. It is absolutely essential that this be the first step of any love relationship. If you don't believe others can love you, you'll believe (probably correctly) that you have no love to give.

It follows that instilling a healthy sense of self-worth is the first step we can take in passing along a realistic view of love to our children. There are a number of ways to do this, but among the most important are:

Remind yourself that the child has a valid point of view and legitimate opinions. Your child may lack maturity, but that does not mean there's any lack of insight on things that matter to him or her. Try to listen now and then, not just issue commands.

Don't tell the child what to feel or what to want. We've already identified this as a condescending and pointless exercise with a partner; the same is true when it comes to children.

Don't belittle the child. The world provides plenty of reasons to criticize oneself; don't spend energy trying to give your child more. Be particularly careful when adolescence dawns and your son or daughter makes his or her first attempts at love. Don't use words like "phase" or "puppy love" in describing these relationships; "experimental" or "awakening" love are better terms.

Don't criticize your child for things he or she cannot change. This can lead to feelings of inadequacy.

Don't force your child to try to excel in areas where he or she has no interest or talent. If there's anything worse than not doing something well, it's being *forced* to do something that you can't do well.

Praise your child's uniqueness in small ways every day. Don't go overboard; do just enough to remind the child that there is no one else exactly like him or her.

Answer your child's questions about sex. If you can help integrate the child's sexuality into his or her personhood, instead of denying that sex exists or compartmentalizing it as an "unmentionable" part of existence, you will have taken a step in the right direction.

We've seen that, in an egalitarian relationship, each partner can depend on a clearly-outlined list of mutual priorities which the partners agree fosters the growth of the relationship and both people in it. There's no reason the same arrangement can't incorporate the children in a family. The items I've outlined above represent a good starting point.

There are few people who can be content with the love of a young child in place of a partner's love. As a rule, marriage partners are lovers before they're parents; affections for one's partner will not disappear the moment a child is born, and nor will needs for support and love.

Thankfully, love is not an inflexible mathematical constant; with a little adjustment to the new environment, most couples discover what worked for two will, in time, make three (or more) very happy.

Perhaps the most difficult part about raising children is identifying where parental authority ends and the child's rights begin. Establishing this elusive point need not be a threatening or unpleasant experience; it can, in fact, lead to mutual respect for privacy and self-determination.

In the end, no matter how hard parents try to communicate honestly and set correct guidelines, they must accept that they will never have absolute control over their child's development, and, indeed, shouldn't try to obtain it. Like it or not, you won't be the only influence your child will encounter.

What, then, should we try to teach our children? That people have two kinds of responsibilities—to themselves, and to others. That we are there for them when they need help growing spiritually and mentally. Finally, that they should love themselves so that they may learn to love others.

Chapter Nine:
Self-Esteem — The Cornerstone

LATELY THERE'S BEEN a flood of books exhorting you to feel good about yourself. Most of them follow a common pattern in the advice they offer. Forget the past, they advise; forget the guilt, just deal with the present. Forget about unpleasant things like sin, retribution, or the fact that you've come down with a terminal illness and have six months to live. Just imagine yourself into a miraculous, joyful existence, forgive everyone who's ever hurt you, accept who you are now, and you'll be all you've ever dreamed of being.

Well, most of this is hogwash. The plain fact is that life, in large measure, is made up of things to worry about. Not only personal things, like family, career, or relationship problems, but also problems relating to the state of the world we live in, a world which must still confront such issues as hunger, overpopulation, torture, the decline of the cities, droughts, floods, famines, and diseases. Try being joyful in the face of all that. It's hard sometimes.

Life can be unfair, unluckly, uninteresting, or unnerving for extended periods of time. Real people, accordingly, have bad moods, periods of depression, and episodes of unrequited love. By the same token, life can also be full of joy, pleasure, and excitement. Even if such experiences are short-lived, they are valid.

The injunction simply to "forgive everyone" is not based in real-life experience. There's no need to be continuously hostile to all those who've hurt you, but for most people the emotional "battle lines" are not so clearly drawn as to allow blanket pardons. Forgiveness is better defined as a direction than an objective. Some people will be easy to forgive; others will have to settle for understanding, rather than complete acceptance; still others will retain a claim on some of our anger, even though we know that hostility, as a rule, uses up too much energy.

I will not ask you to pretend that yours is the only reality, or that you live in a perfect world. My message is this: Though you must acknowledge the pain of the real world, you can renew and revitalize yourself by being helpful to others and by reaching out beyond your own pain.

Sometimes, to be sure, you will feel guilty. If you do something wrong (as any human being will) try to learn from your mistakes and remedy the situation to the best of your ability. Then drop it. Try not to make the mistake of feeling guilty irrationally or punishing yourself beyond reason. Accept yourself. In time, you will acquire wisdom without even trying. In time, you'll become comfortable with a healthy level of daydreaming about your future, and you'll spend less time castigating yourself. And in time, you'll be willing to take risks with others. Each of these achievements will open up exciting new possibilities for you.

Feeling Good About Yourself:
What It Doesn't Mean

Watch out for people who feel so good about themselves that they have no qualms whatsoever about riding roughshod over the feelings of others.

Trying to feel good about yourself should not become an

excuse for selfish, greedy, or uncaring behavior. You'd be surprised how many people come away from the new age, cure-yourself, you-are-your-own-salvation workshops feeling "good" about themselves and being just plain mean to everybody else. That's not the kind of "feeling good" I mean. The kind I'm talking about leaves you with more energy, higher levels of optimism, and a willingness to be nice to the majority of the people with whom you come in contact.

Obviously, there's more to developing healthy levels of self-esteem than trying to spend most of the day ecstatically happy. (If that were the case, drug abusers, who can experience brief periods of ecstasy when high, would be the happiest people on earth.) Human beings have ups and downs. Well-adjusted people will feel depressed when something depressing happens. But they won't be "married" to the depression or allow themselves to fixate on how awful the world is for days on end. They'll get through it.

Such people have usually developed what's called "self-acceptance"—the ability to distinguish rational from irrational thoughts, and, most important, the ability to separate one's behavior from the acceptance of oneself as a person.

To be self-accepting, you must believe that you are basically good. You must believe that to be a human is a positive experience, and that no human being on earth – *including you* – is inherently bad.

To be sure, humans are fallible. We make mistakes. It's up to us to turn those mistakes into lessons. If we've experienced a failure, such as a marriage that didn't work out, we recognize the reality of the situation. The marriage failed. But a self-accepting person will know that the fact that the marriage was a failure is no indication that the *people* involved are now failures.

Ten:
Summing Up

IT'S THE END of the book . . . but perhaps you still have doubts.

That's all right. No one claimed that finding and keeping a mature relationship was an exact science. There will be times you feel uncertain about what you should do next.

Thankfully, there are basic guidelines you can follow. The first one is simple: Do you love yourself? Are you gentle with yourself? Are you making a habit of proceeding from the idea that you're worth spending time with?

Secondly, about your relationships with others . . . there are questions you can ask about the relationship, observations you can make that will help you determine whether or not you're on the right track.

If you find that your partner consistently makes you feel bad about yourself, and that you have to spend the rest of the day recovering from the damage, then you've received a clear signal that you're involved in an immature relationship. Similarly, if you feel good about yourself *only* in the presence of your partner, or seem, as a result of the relationship, not to care about the rest of the world or the feelings of others, the odds are good that the relationship is not going to make you happy in the long term.

But if you're in the kind of relationship that makes you feel good about yourself both when you're with your partner and when you're apart; the kind of relationship that reinforces your acceptance of yourself without draining every bit of energy from your mate; the kind of relationship that leaves you feeling happy at the end of the day, as though you'd found your place in the world . . . then congratulations. You're involved in a challenging, growth-oriented, mature relationship.

Keep growing!

The Secret

Permit me to conclude with an autobiographical note.

I'm past sixty-five years old; I'm far from retiring. I travel around the country; people say I give very animated lectures. I'm often asked, "Where on earth do you get all that energy?"

I'll let you in on my secret.

When I began my professional career about forty years ago, I was out to save the world. I tried that for a few years, without much success. I was getting depressed about it; eventually I came to the conclusion that I might have taken on too much.

So I decided to save the United States.

After a few years of intense work I didn't have much to show for my efforts. I was crestfallen. Had I been on the wrong track from the very beginning? I resolved to save my neighborhood.

My neighbors didn't appreciate my zeal. Furious, they usually told me to mind my own business.

I considered the possibility of going to Harvard to earn an MBA.

I decided I wasn't that desperate yet. I vowed to redouble my efforts and work on saving my own family.

I had to accept, finally, that I was having a hard time doing that.

Through all the experiences, I learned something about humility. I learned that I couldn't be a hero in somebody else's situation. I could only be me in my situation.

Sometimes, when I get depressed, I turn to the Talmud (a commentary on the Old Testament). One day, as I was reading, a miracle took place.

As though written for me, the Talmud proclaimed, "If you can save one person, it's as though you've saved the world."

One person. One at a time.

That's my secret. That's the key to leading a meaningful life and having more than enough energy.

If this book "saves" one person, makes the world a little easier to live in for only one reader, it will have served its purpose. And I will have done my mitzvah.

If you're the reader I've helped, so much the better. Now it's your turn. Do a mitzvah. Don't ask anyone's permission (they'll just say no). Just do it.

And you know what else is nice about mitzvah therapy?

You meet the nicest people along the way.

Bibliography

Recommended Reading

Herewith, some of the most helpful books I've come across dealing with the topics of self-esteem, relationships, sexuality, and long-term personal growth. If you have time or desire to read only ten books over the next year, reach for the stars (*); I've placed asterisks by the ten books I consider absolutely essential.

Barbach, Lonnie
For Each Other: Sharing Sexual Intimacy
Signet, 1984

Berman, Claire
Preparing To Remarry
Public Affairs Pamphlet, 1987

Bessell, Harold
The Love Test
Warner, 1984

Bienvenu, Millard
Strengthen Your Marriage
Through Better Communication
Public Affairs Pamphlet, 1986

Boston Women's Health Book Collective
*The New Our Bodies, Our Selves**
Simon & Schuster, 1984

Buscaglia, Leo
Living, Loving, and Learning
Fawcett, 1983

Carnes, P.
The Sexual Addiction
Compcare, 1983

Cassell, Carol
Swept Away:
Why Women Fear Their Own Sexuality*
Bantam, 1985

Cohen, Sara Kay
Whoever Said Life Was Fair?
A Guide to Growing Through Life's Injustices
Berkley, 1984

Colton, Helen
Touch Therapy
Zebra, 1985

Comfort, Alex
More Joy of Sex
Crown, 1987

Cowan, Connel, and Kinder, Melvyn
Women Men Love—Women Men Leave
Signet, 1987

Crewsdon, J.
By Silence Betrayed:
Sexual Abuse of Children in America
Little Brown, 1988

Dodson, Betty
Sex for One: The Joy of Selfloving
Crown, 1987

Ellis, Albert
How To Stubbornly Refuse To Make Yourself Miserable About Anything—Yes, Anything*
Lyle Stuart, 1988

Ellis, Albert, and Harper, Robert
The New Guide to Rational Living
Wilshire, 1977

Farrell, Warren
Why Men Are The Way They Are
Berkley, 1988

Fischer, Joel, and Gochros, Harvey
Treat Yourself to a Better Sex Life
Prentice-Hall, 1980

Frankl, Victor
Man's Search for Meaning*
Touchstone, 1984

Friday, Nancy
Jealousy
William Morrow, 1985

Friedan, Betty
The Second Stage
Summit, 1981

Friedman, Sonia
Smart Cookies Don't Crumble
Pocket, 1985

Fromm, Erich
The Art of Loving
Bantam, 1956

Gaylin, Willard
Rediscovering Love
Penguin, 1987

Gordon, Sol
Seduction Lines Heard 'Round the World and Answers You Can Give
Prometheus, 1987

Gordon, Sol
*When Living Hurts**
Dell, 1988

Gordon, Sol and Gordon, Judith
Raising a Child Conservatively in a Sexually Permissive World
Fireside, 1986

Gordon, Sol, and Snyder, Craig
Personal Issues in Human Sexuality (2nd edition)
Allyn & Bacon, 1989

Grant, Toni
Being a Woman: Fulfilling Your Femininity
Random House, 1988

Greenberg, Martin
The Birth of a Father
Avon, 1986

Harayda, Janice
The Joy of Being Single
Doubleday, 1986

Hazelton, L.
The Right to Feel Bad: Coming to Terms with Normal Depression*
Dial Press, 1984

Hoffman, Susanna
Men Who Are Good For You And Men Who Are Bad
Ten Speed Press, 1987

Jampolsky, Gerald
Love Is Letting Go of Fear
Bantam, 1981

Kelly, Garry
Learning About Sex: The Contemporary Guide for Young Adults
Barron's, 1987

Kennedy, Eugene
A Time For Love
Image Books, 1972

Klagsbrun, F.
Married People: Staying Together in the Age of Divorce
Bantam, 1985

Klein, Marty
Sexual Secrets
E.P. Dutton, 1988

Kushner, Harold S.
When Bad Things Happen to Good People*
Avon, 1983

Lasswell, Marcia, and Lobsenz, Norman
Styles of Loving
Ballantine, 1984

Lazarus, Arnold A.
Marital Myths
Impact, 1985

Leight, Lynn
Raising Your Child to Be Sexually Healthy
Rawson, 1988

Masters and Johnson, with Levin
The Pleasure Bond: A New Look at Sexuality and Commitment
Little Brown, 1975

Masters and Johnson, with Kolodny
On Sex and Human Loving
Little Brown, 1986

McCarthy, B. and E.
Sexual Awareness: Enhancing Sexual Pleasure
Carroll & Graff, 1984

McCoy, Kathleen
Coping With Single Parenting
NAL, 1987

McNaught, Brian
On Being Gay
St. Martins, 1988

Nelson, James B.
Between Two Gardens:
Reflections on Sexuality and Religious Experience
Pilgrim Press, 1988

Nelson, James B.
The Intimate Connection: Male Sexuality, Masculine Spirituality
Westminster Press, 1988

Norwood, Robin
Women Who Love Too Much
Pocket, 1986

Olds, S.W.
The Eternal Garden: Secrets of Our Sexuality
Times, 1985

Parrot, Andrea
Coping with Date Rape and Acquaintance Rape
Rosen Publishing, 1988

Paul, Jordan and Margaret
Do I Have to Give Up Me to Be Loved by You?
Compcare, 1985

Paul, Jordan and Margaret, with Bonnie Hesse
If You Really Loved Me. . .
Compcare, 1987

Peck, M. Scott
The Different Drum
Simon & Schuster, 1987

Peck, M. Scott
The Road Less Traveled*
Simon & Schuster, 1978

Pogrebin, L.
Among Friends
McGraw-Hill, 1987

Prather, Hugh and Gayle
  Book for Couples
  Doubleday, 1988

Raphael, Sally Jessy
  Finding Love
  Jove, 1988

Scanzoni, L.D.
  Sexuality
  Westminster Press, 1984

Schaeffer, Brenda
  Is It Love Or Is It Addiction?
  Harper/Hazelden, 1987

Schiff, Eilleen (Ed.)
  *Experts Advise Parents**
  Delacorte, 1988

Smedes, Lewis B.
  *Forgive and Forget**
  Pocket, 1986

Sullivan, S.K., and Kawiak, M.A.
  Parents Talk Love: A Family Handbook About Sexuality
  Bantam, 1988

Twerski, Abraham
  Like Yourself and Others Will, Too
  Prentice-Hall, 1986

Viorst, Judith
  Necessary Losses
  Fawcett, 1986

Westheimer, Ruth, and Lieberman, Louis
Sex and Morality
HBJ, 1988

Zilbergeld, B.
Male Sexuality
Bantam, 1988

Index

ABOUT THE AUTHOR

Dr. Sol Gordon, who has been a professor of Child and Family Studies at Syracuse University, is a nationally-noted author, lecturer, and educator. His previous works include WHEN LIVING HURTS and the Paramount video, HOW CAN I TELL IF I'M REALLY IN LOVE? He is an internationally-praised writer on a number of important topics, including suicide prevention, sexuality, and personal development.